"AND SO TO BED"

"AND SO TO BED"

(AN ADVENTURE WITH PEPYS)

A Comedy in Three Acts

BY

J. B. FAGAN

SAMUEL FRENCH

LONDON

NEW YORK SYDNEY TORONTO HOLLYWOOD

"AND SO TO BED"

Produced under the management of the author at the Queen's Theatre, London, W.C., on Monday, the 6th September, 1926, transferred to the Savoy Theatre on the 1st November, 1926, and to the Globe Theatre on 1st May, 1927, with the following cast of characters (in the order of their appearance):

SUE	Gwen Harter.
BOY TO PEPYS	Lewis Shaw.
SAMUEL PEPYS	Edmund Gwenn.
DOLL (a Blackamoor)	Emma Williams.
MRS. KNIGHT	Mary Grey.
A WATCHMAN	Edmund Gordon.
JULIA	Mignon O'Doherty.
PELLING (the Potticary)	Alfred Clark.
PELHAM HUMFREY	Ivan Samson.
CÆSAR	D. Poulton.
MRS. PIERCE	Kitty de Legh.
MRS. KNEPP	Gwendolen Evans.
MRS. PEPYS	Yvonne Arnaud.
LETTICE	Betty Price.
PRODGERS (Groom of the Bedchamber)	Reginald Smith.
CHARLES II	Allan Jeayes.

The Play produced by the AUTHOR.

PERIOD.—A few days after the close of the *Diary*, June, 1669. The action covers 8 hours.

PLACE.—London.

N.B.—"Mrs." should be spoken as "Mistress" throughout the play.

ACT I
A room in PEPYS' House.

ACT II
MRS. KNIGHT'S Lodging in Gray's Inn Fields.

ACT III
A room in PEPYS' House.

"AND SO TO BED"

ACT I

SCENE.—*A room in* PEPYS' *House in Seething* Lane. *Stairs leading to gallery* R., *under them a passage leading to street entrance. Below them door to kitchen, etc. The* L. *wall is hung half-way up with tapestries ; in the* C. *of it a deeply embrasured Tudor window. Above the tapestries hang the portraits of* PEPYS *and his wife by* Hales. *Behind the hangings are shelves and books, etc., and music. A long Cromwellian table* L., *with stools on either side and a chair at either end. At the side of the stairs a chest, above this bookshelves with a cupboard below. Door to* PEPYS' *bedroom on the gallery above. A triangular scene.*

(SUE *is discovered seated on oak chest* R., *polishing the silver candlesticks and tankards, and singing at her work. A few minutes later the outside door is heard closing and* PEPYS' BOY *enters* R.C., *carrying a satchel and a parcel of books, which he lays on the table.* PEPYS *follows, grave, businesslike, laconic.* SUE *rises. The* BOY *takes his hat.* PEPYS *stands silent a moment, then goes to the cupboard behind the tapestry, from which he takes four loose sheets of paper. He folds them and gives them to the* BOY.)

PEPYS. See that these schedules be left for Mr. Creed at the Navy Office by six of the clock.

BOY. Yes, master.

PEPYS. If Robert Williams come to the door I am not in. If he ask when, say never, so long as the rope he sells to the yards be short of weight and rotten besides.

BOY. Yes, master.

PEPYS. Bid Doll here to me.

(BOY *goes out down* R. PEPYS *stands watching* SUE, *who is putting the silver back in the chest.*)

How old art now, Sue ?

SUE. Seventeen come midsummer, sir.

PEPYS (*coming over*). And a mighty pretty sprightly jade, too. (*Holding up her chin.*) Those cherries be ripe that hang temptingly under that nose.

5

SUE. Forbidden fruit, sir.
PEPYS. The sweeter for that! (*Kissing her.*)
SUE. Oh, sir!
PEPYS. Wast ever kist before, Sue?
SUE. Oh, no, sir!
PEPYS. Pretty liar!

(*He is about to kiss her again when the* BOY *returns and goes upstairs with hat and stick.* PEPYS *turns away.*)

Fetch the six pairs of old shoes, girl, from the corner of my closet, and make me a stout parcel for the carrier to Brampton to my father.
SUE. I will, sir.

(*She goes upstairs and out.*)

PEPYS (*to himself*). He did desire me to send them; and yet it is a thing against my mind to have him wear my old shoes. (*Picking up a big book from the table.*) A Bible for ten pounds, and worth forty! (*Picking up two small books.*) Another play . . . and yet another! When will I make an end of plays!

(*He takes the Bible and goes with the books to the bookcase.* DOLL *enters* R.)

Where is your mistress, Doll?
DOLL. She be gone to Deptford, in de new coach, to see her mother.
PEPYS. What time went she forth?
DOLL. 'Bout noon, massa.
PEPYS. She cannot be back before dark, so supper at nine. (*Going to cupboard.*)
DOLL. Yes, massa.
PEPYS. And where are your week's accounts? 'Tis Tuesday, and on Sunday I should have them.
DOLL. Wid all dose people comin' I never had de time to——
PEPYS (*rapping the table*). Make an end of words, woman, and bring me your accounts!

(DOLL *hurries out down* R. : PEPYS *moving around to behind table, takes from the cupboard some loose sheets of music and a flageolet. He sits at the head of the table and begins playing the obligato to "Beauty Retire." He plays five or six bars, then alters a note with the pen and begins again. Suddenly a scream is heard from a woman's voice in the street outside, then a gruff voice.*)

MAN'S VOICE. Now, my lady madam, give me that bag!
MAID'S VOICE. Help! Thieves! Murder! Help!

MAN'S VOICE. Peace, you bawling trull!

(*The sound of a blow, then the* MAID'S *voice screaming as she runs away.*)

The bag, quick, and we part friends!

LADY'S VOICE. Begone, rogue, begone!

(PEPYS, *who at the first sound of trouble has laid down his flageolet and sat nervously listening, now goes cautiously to the window.*)

MAN'S VOICE. Give me the bag, or I'll break your pretty neck!

LADY'S VOICE. Rascal! Help! Help!

PEPYS (*throwing open the window*). Ruffian! Unhand the lady!
(*Shaking his fist.*) Wait till I come at you!

LADY'S VOICE. Help! Help! Oh!

PEPYS (*shouting up the stairs*). Boy! Jacke! (*Then out of the window.*) Villain! Begone, or by Heaven I'll—— (*To the* BOY, *who has rushed on from above.*) Quick, boy, into the street! A ruffian robbing a pretty lady on my very threshold! On! On! While I arm against him!

(*He rushes about looking for something to throw, sees the pewter mug by the settle and runs with it to the window, while the* BOY *rushes out.*)

Let go the lady, you lousy coward! (*Flinging the pewter pot, which rattles down the street.*)

MAN'S VOICE. I'll leave you the wench when I've plucked her!

PEPYS (*shaking his fist*). You shall hang for it! As sure as my name is Samuel Pepys you shall hang! (*Suddenly bending forward and shouting.*) Hey! Watch! This way, quick! Seize the ruffian! Come on! (*Seeing a crockery pot and picking it up.*) Run him down! Raise the hue and cry! Stop thief, stop thief! (*Flinging the pot.*) Ah, ruffian, wait till I catch thee!

(*The pot crashes on the street.* SUE *is at the top of the stairs looking out of the window;* DOLL *stands gaping in terror at door* R.)

BOY'S VOICE. The lady's swooned, sir!

PEPYS. In a swoon, sweet creature! Hey! Watch! Help my boy to bear the lady in!

WATCHMAN'S VOICE. Ay, ay, sir!

PEPYS. So, so! And for the ruffian who ran from me, I shall know him again, I warrant you! (*Leaving the window.*) Sue, a bowl of water—haste, haste!

(SUE *exits above and returns later with a bowl of water.*)

(*To* DOLL.) Fetch me a goose feather and a taper. (*Clapping his hands.*) Run, you gaping slut you!

(DOLL *runs off* R. *front. He goes to entrance* R.)

So! Gently, gently!

(*The* WATCHMAN *enters, with* MRS. KNIGHT *leaning on his shoulder, the* BOY *supporting her on the other side.*)

Set her here. . . . Run, boy, a bottle of the old sack to revive her.

(*The* BOY *runs out up* R. PEPYS *and the* WATCHMAN *support* MRS. KNIGHT *to chair* R. *end of table.*)

Now, fellow, after that rogue and apprehend him!

WATCHMAN. Ay, ay! Leave him to me!

PEPYS. Run, fellow, run! (*Then taking a handful of water, sprinkles her face, dipping handkerchief in bowl of water, sits with his arm round her dabbing her forehead.*)

WATCHMAN (*folding his cloak about him*). No hurry, sir. I'll lay him prettily by the heels, or my name ain't Solomon Gumbridge. (*Going out slowly.*)

PEPYS (*gazing at* MRS. KNIGHT *and mopping her forehead*). A mighty fine fair lady, i' faith. Why did I not kill the rogue! (*To* DOLL, *who enters with a lighted taper and a goose quill.*) Here, wench! (*Burning the feather and holding it smoking under* MRS. KNIGHT'S *nose.*) A sovereign remedy, egad! A foul stink of burnt feathers and a smell of roast goose would raise the dead to life. (*As* MRS. KNIGHT *moves her head and sighs.*) She sighs!

(*The* BOY *brings on a bottle and glass and puts them on the table.* PEPYS *shakes the feather under the lady's nose again.*)

MRS. KNIGHT. Oh, sir!

PEPYS. That's better! (*To* SUE.) 'Tis well, girl.

(SUE *goes upstairs with the basin. He waves to* DOLL, *who goes out. Sitting on the table edge, he takes a glass of sack from the* BOY, *who goes out.*)

Drink this, madam.

MRS. KNIGHT. Where am I?

PEPYS. In a safe place, madam—don't move.

MRS. KNIGHT. Oh . . . (*Looking up.*)

PEPYS. Eyes mighty fine (*aside*). (*Giving her drink.*) Another sup—old sack, and full of good cheer. (*As she sighs again.*) He has not hurt you?

MRS. KNIGHT. No, no, not hurt, only frightened. I begin to be myself again. (*Looking at him as he puts the glass on the table.*) And so it was you who saved me?

PEPYS (*deprecatingly with a wave of his hand*). 'Twas nothing, madam. A mere nothing.

MRS. KNIGHT. Oh, but indeed——

PEPYS (*bowing to her*). Beauty in distress—nothing, madam, I assure you.

Mrs. Knight. Nothing ! He might have killed me. I owe you my life !

Pepys (*swaggering*). Faith, I made him run, and that's the truth ! He spied danger in my eye, fear prodded him behind, and he saved his life by taking to his heels.

Mrs. Knight. As modest as you are brave !

Pepys. Simple truth, madam. The coward gave me no time to kill him. Had he stayed a moment longer his corpse were rotting now below my window.

Mrs. Knight (*suddenly realizing her loss*). My bag ! He hath got my bag——

Pepys. Bag ?

Mrs. Knight. With thirty pounds in gold——

Pepys (*crossing* R. *of her*). Pestilent villain !

Mrs. Knight (*feeling her ears*). And my ear-rings—— !

Pepys. Alas, madam, I saw nothing——

Mrs. Knight. And my pearls—— !

Pepys. I saw only blood : (*describing the imaginary fight*) blow and counterblow—crack, crack—and blind with fury till I perceived the knave was gone.

Mrs. Knight (*turning to* Pepys). And I speak of trifles to one who has just risked his life to save me. Indeed I know not how I can thank you.

Pepys. By not speaking of it, madam. But may I not know to whom I have had the fortune to render a trifling service ?

Mrs. Knight. I am Mistress Knight.

Pepys (*bowing*). Madam! (*Suddenly, as he remembers.*) Not Mistress Knight the singer ?

Mrs. Knight. The same, at your service.

Pepys. Faith, here's a rare coincidence !

Mrs. Knight. Coincidence ?

Pepys. Near two year ago I was brought to your lodging to hear you sing, but you were away, and so I missed you : till t'other day I was told of you again and vowed I'd never rest till I had heard you.

Mrs. Knight. So I have robbed you of your rest, sir ?

Pepys. Faith, music I could live and die for.

Mrs. Knight. And who is this music lover to whom I owe my life ?

Pepys (*bowing*). Samuel Pepys, madam, and your most humble servant.

Mrs. Knight. Pepys ! Not *the* Mr. Pepys ?

Pepys. Why, truly there be some—many, indeed, would speak thus. . . . And at the Navy Office——

Mrs. Knight. Oh, I have heard of you, never fear !

Pepys. But when shall *I* hear you sing ?

Mrs. Knight. Nay, since you cannot rest——

PEPYS. I'faith——

MRS. KNIGHT. To-night.

PEPYS. To-night! . . . Where?

MRS. KNIGHT. At my lodging.

PEPYS. I have forgot the place——

MRS. KNIGHT. I will write it for you.

(*She writes with pen on a slip of paper on the table.* PEPYS *stands over her.*)

(*Giving him the paper.*) So!

PEPYS (*reading*). " Willow House, North Side, Gray's Inn Fields " I shall be there. (*Pocketing the paper.*) At what hour, ma'am? (*Sitting on a stool near her, on her* L.)

MRS. KNIGHT. After seven. A half-hour after.

PEPYS. I shall be there—to the minute.

MRS. KNIGHT (*picking up a sheet of music*). Why, 'tis music!

PEPYS. 'Tis the thing of the world I love most.

MRS. KNIGHT. I wonder. . . . (*Reading.*) " ' Beauty Retire,' etcetera, being set to music by Samuel Pepys." You write songs?

PEPYS. A few pretty well—but this mighty fine.

MRS. KNIGHT. Then to-night I shall sing it.

PEPYS. And to-night I shall play it with you on my flageolet.

MRS. KNIGHT. You play the flageolet?

PEPYS. Ay, faith! . . . (*Boastfully.*) I play on many instruments.

MRS. KNIGHT. Indeed!

PEPYS (*taking her hand.*) And to-night we may make mighty pretty music together—you and I.

(*He kisses her hand. The* BOY *enters at arch up* R.)

BOY. Sir, there is a waiting-woman at the door, who asks for a Mistress Knight.

MRS. KNIGHT. 'Tis Julia, my runaway maid.

PEPYS. Bid her in.

(*The* BOY *goes off.*)

MRS. KNIGHT. The fool ran for help, or fright, at the first blow. (*Rising as* JULIA *comes in carrying a bandbox.*) So, my valorous wench, at last! How many times have you bravely sworn that you would die for me, and at the first proof you show your heels like a Welsh hare! What have you to say?

JULIA. Thank the Lord you're safe, ma'am.

MRS. KNIGHT. Thank Mr. Pepys, Julia, and no thanks to you!

JULIA (*dropping an unwilling curtsy to* PEPYS). I have a coach at the door, madam. We walk no more in these back alleys and crooked lanes.

MRS. KNIGHT. Curb your tongue, malapert ! And go on before me !

(JULIA *goes off. She holds her hand out to* PEPYS.)

A rivederci, my lover . . . of music ! I shall expect you half an hour after seven.

PEPYS (*holding and stroking her hand*). Expect me on the stroke of the clock, madam.

MRS. KNIGHT. Nay, but 'tis my hand you are stroking !

PEPYS. 'Tis to pass the time till then.

MRS. KNIGHT (*with a laugh*). And my coach is waiting——

PEPYS. Not half as impatiently as I. (*Kissing her hand.*)

MRS. KNIGHT (*crossing, laughing*). Come, Mr. Pepys. Help me to my coach, or I shall suspect your impatience to hear me sing !

PEPYS. Madam, I am above suspicion.

(*She sails out laughing, followed by* PEPYS. SUE *comes down the stairs with a bundle and goes into the kitchen. The door shuts and the rumble of a departing coach is heard.* PEPYS *returns, rubbing his hands.*)

(*Standing at the open window, looking out.*) A merry lady as ever I saw in my life ! . . . Away in her coach ! And a leg ! The shapeliest I ever saw, God forgive me ! . . . (*With a kiss of his hand, turning from the window as he closes it.*) She shall have green stockings. (*Coming down to his chair.*) Ay, there is no salvation for a leg save in green stockings. . . . She shall be saved !

(*He takes up his flageolet.* DOLL *enters from door down* R. *carrying a hare.*)

DOLL. Massa Pelling's compliments, an' dis hare, an' he say he give himself de pleasure to sup with you to-night !

PEPYS. He shall and welcome. (*Looking up.*) A hare ! Faith, that's mighty strange ! Here with it on the table, wench.

(DOLL *lays it on the table.*)

Look at that ! (*Taking a hare's foot from his pocket.*) For two months I have carried this hare's foot against the colic, and been in good plight—whether it be that, or my taking every morning a pill of turpentine, I know not—till Sunday night after supper, pain and mighty rumbling within.

DOLL. La bless you, massa, dat was de pork. . . . I said dere 'ud be trouble in de house over dat pork !

PEPYS. Well, this morning comes me Mr. Batten in Westminster Hall, shows me his hare's foot, and that mine hath no virtue since it has not the joint to it. (*Taking a knife from his pocket.*) So now I'll have the hind leg of this fellow and eat what I please. (*Cutting off the leg.*)

DOLL. La sakes, dat lil' old hare some good, eh ? (*Laughing.*)

PEPYS. I think I be a fool to set store by it, but fancy is a mighty fine physic. (*Puts the new leg in his pocket and throws her the old one.*) Give that one to the cat. Take your three-legged hare and give me your account.

DOLL (*giving him a paper*). Up to de night ob Sunday mornin', massa.

PEPYS (*reading at first in a murmur, then more and more loudly*). A chine of beef of sixteen pounds. A quarter of mutton. A barrel of oysters. Five capons and thirty-six eggs. A goose. Chine of beef of twenty-one pounds. Another of twenty-eight pounds. Three barrels of oysters. A goose. A goose for roasting. Another goose. Ten small pullets and sixty eggs. Chine of beef of thirty-six pounds ! ! ! (*Rising and exploding.*) What a plague, woman ! Have you eaten ninety-nine pounds of beef ? Eight—ten—twelve dozen eggs ? Birds by the score, and a *bed* of oysters ? Monstrous ! Monstrous ! (*Moving down* L.)

DOLL. Oh, go 'way, massa ! Why you feedin' all dose people every night at supper ?

PEPYS (*coming again to* DOLL *and shaking the paper in her face*). But not feeding the army, woman, not victualling the fleet ! Waste, monstrous waste and extravagance !

DOLL. All dose Turners, an' Bateliers, an' Massa Gibson, an'—an'——

PEPYS. Slight feeders all of them !

DOLL. An' singin' men—an'—an'——

PEPYS. Waste, woman, waste in kitchen and court and every office in the country ! Zoons, trollop ! Ninety-nine pounds of beef ! Enough to make a man mad !

DOLL (*taking up the hare*). An' I cook de lil' ole hare for supper ?

PEPYS. Ay, that—and perhaps a breast of veal, roasted, with a ham of bacon to it.

DOLL. Sartin' I will.

PEPYS. And I fancy too a loin of mutton fried, with that sauce of onions my wife dotes on. And for the fish——

(DOLL, *who has been going, turns.*)

—a barrel of oysters—a jowl of salmon—or two lobsters—or both. . . . Supper at nine. . . . I have mightily to do—in the King's business—before them. For the pastry and kickshaws, what you please, but everything proper for an extraordinary good handsome supper.

(*Enter* BOY. DOLL *goes out* R.)

Well, sirrah ?

BOY. Mr. Pelling has been waiting without, sir, and——

PEPYS. Bid him in, bid him in ! Zoons, d'ye know no better than to keep my friend Pelling waiting ?

(*The* BOY *runs out, and* PELLING *enters immediately.   He is a mournfully merry nut-cracker of a man, dressed in black.*)

Good morrow, Pelling !

PELLING.   I brought you a hare, Mr. Pepys, to ask if I might sup with you.

PEPYS.   And I answered him you were welcome.

PELLING.   And the hare has a tale !

PEPYS.   Let it wag !

PELLING.   Little Pelham Humfrey is newly come from France.

PEPYS (*moving to above the table, followed by* PELLING *to the head of the table*).   And a mighty good musician as I hear. . . . You'll drink a glass with me ?   (*Calling.*) Boy ! Another glass ! A fine musician ; they say the king hath paid for him abroad to study. (*Both sitting at the table.*)

PELLING.   These three years.   He has all the newest modes. He was with Lulli in Paris. . . .   In fine, he is coming here to meet you at my bidding, and at yours we may have him to sup and make music to-night.

PEPYS.   Nothing could content me better.

(*The* BOY *has placed another glass on the table and gone out.*)

I am a glutton for music, i' faith. . . .   Come, this will put new blood in you. (*Filling the glasses.*) Music and wine, and but one thing wanting. . . . (*Drinking.*) Here go my good resolutions. Is it not odd, Pelling, that a man will make vows at New Year, and write 'em down, and read 'em daily, and break 'em every day of the year ?   Why is it ?

PELLING.   Original sin. (*Drinking.*)

PEPYS.   'Tis damned unoriginal by now, i' faith. What's the news with you ?

PELLING.   All the news of the town, and not worth the telling. . . . (*Taking a sheet of music from his pocket.*) But this *is* new. . . . Pelham bade me give it you. 'Tis a minuet of Lulli's, in his own hand.

(PEPYS *examines it, blinking and holding it away from him, humming a few bars, with difficulty.*)

PEPYS (*laying it down*).   I cannot well read the pricking of these notes.   Toward evening my eyes do ache terribly. (*Takes from his pocket a pair of horn-rimmed green glasses and continues humming the air.*) Ay, pretty well—light and fanciful. But I cannot hold that the French have better than our English tunes.

PELLING.   'Tis the fashion to say so.

PEPYS (*nodding*).   Lord, how it vexes me to hear how we cry up their tunes and their clothes and their women. Give me an English song, an English cloth, an English wench before all their fripperies. (*Taking off his glasses and putting same with song on the table.*) But

I would my eyes did mend. The great light hurts them—candles most—I find a comfort in these. (*Touching his spectacles.*) But I do live in a mighty fear of blindness. To be all dark . . . to lose the merry picture of life, not to see a play again, nor a pretty woman smile. . . . Slow starving to death—Lord help me ! (*Drains his wine and refills his own glass.*)

PELLING (*tapping his glass*). Moderation is the Lord's help, Mr. Pepys.

PEPYS. Ay. I am greedy of life . . . all of it. I make vows, I fine myself to the poor—but God knows my devil that is within me will have his way. I cannot keep from a play or a pretty woman while I have eyes to see 'em. Why are we made so, Pelling ?

PELLING. By too much drinking, by too good eating, they think.

PEPYS. Do they so ? May be. Drink !—I know the devil is in it—but eating ? Think you beef may be the cause of kissing ?

PELLING (*nodding*). Meat, they think, to be a great inflamer of the passions.

PEPYS. Faith, then, Solomon's seven hundred concubines were scarce enough for the beef our cookmaid charged me with to-day. But no wine from to-morrow—(*drains his glass*)—for a while.

PELLING. Do these glasses save the eyes ?

PEPYS. A little, but they save my mind a lot. (*Chuckling.*)

PELLING. How mean you ?

PEPYS. Faith, I'll tell you. When my wife, poor wretch, is jealous and questions me too close (*putting on glasses*) I put them on so she cannot see in my eyes what my thoughts would be at. Which contents me mightily, may the Lord forgive me. (*Takes off glasses and puts them in pocket, from which he takes the piece of paper.*)

PELLING. I thank the Lord I am a bachelor.

PEPYS. Nay, she is the best wife i' the world to me. I love her dearly. The house seems hell when she is abroad—and a hellish sort of heaven when she is home, i' faith. (*He hands* PELLING *the paper given him by* MRS. KNIGHT.) Do you remember the house that is writ there ?

(PELLING *stares at it.*)

You took me near on two years ago.

PELLING (*reading*). "Willow House—North Side, Gray's Inn Fields." Why—'tis where Mistress Knight used to lodge.

PEPYS (*nodding*). And we went to hear her sing, and she was out and so we lost our pains.

PELLING. I remember . . . before she went to Italy.

PEPYS. Egad. I am to hear her sing now, Pelling, by her own invitation.

PELLING. You are acquainted ? (*Lays the paper on the table before him.*)

PEPYS. Yes, faith—a chance meeting . . . (PELLING *drinks*) a

trifling . . . service I did her . . . it happened, well . . . to tell
you the truth, I saved her life (PELLING *puts down his glass and turns
suddenly to* PEPYS) . . . a ruffian who would have robbed and murdered her. And when I had half killed and chased the rogue, she,
sweet creature, was all tears, all thanks, and so—one day we are
to make music together. . . . A mighty fine fair lady . . . I shall
take my flageolet, 'twill suit well with her voice.

PELLING. You are to be envied, she sings like an angel—a voice
that brought even the King to her feet.

PEPYS. The King!

PELLING. Ay, indeed.

PEPYS. With Mistress Knight?

PELLING. They said in those days he was mightily took with
her.

PEPYS. A common mistress to the King, say you?

PELLING. They said so . . . did you not know it?

PEPYS (*rising*). Never, as I live.

PELLING. 'Twas His Majesty, they say, sent her into Italy.

PEPYS (*striding about indignant*). 'Tis enough (*moving* R.) to
make a man mad. Is there no end to it? (*Coming back to* C. *to* L.)
Is there no fruit he hath not fingered? (*Moving down* R.) Lord,
to think the state we are in, with the King minding nothing but
his pleasures (*turning and going up stage*), thinking only of women,
and hating the very sight or thought of business! (*Moving to back
of table.*) And the Queen, poor soul, neglected . . . slighted in the
face of all England. It makes me mad.

(*The* BOY *enters* R.C.)

Well, rogue, speak. What is it?

BOY. If you please, sir, Mr. Pelham Humfrey and Mr. Cæsar to
wait on you.

PEPYS (*at chair* R. *of table*). Bid them in, bid them in!

(*The* BOY *goes out.*)

(PELLING *rises, lays the music sheet which he has been looking at on
the card.*)

PELLING (*crossing down* L.). And now we shall have some music?

PEPYS. And now I am not in the mood for it.

(*The* BOY *shows in* PELHAM HUMFREY, *a handsome dapper youth,
somewhat over-dressed in French fashion, and carrying a cithern
in a bag of green silk, followed by* MR. WILLIAM CÆSAR, *a middle-
aged man, soberly dressed, who carries a lute.*)

PELLING. You come in good time, Mr. Humfrey. Let me present
you to Mr. Pepys.

B

HUMFREY.   Mr. Pepys, *votre serviteur.*   (*With an exaggerated bow.*)
I am charmed to make your acquaintance.

PEPYS.   Your servant, Mr. Humfrey.   Friend Cæsar, how do ye ?

CÆSAR.   Faith, I don't complain, Mr. Pepys.

PELLING.   Mr. Pepys is musician to his soul, plays, sings, com-
poses . . .

HUMFREY.   Oh, I have heard . . . I have heard . . . (*Moving
down* R.)

PEPYS.   Boy, more burgundy and glasses.

HUMFREY.   Pray not for me !

PEPYS.   You drink no wine ?

HUMFREY.   I drink no wine but *champagne.* (*With the French
pronunciation.*)

PEPYS.   I'gad we have none o' that for I never heard of it.   A
glass of ale for Mr. Cæsar . . . I know his taste.

(*The* BOY *goes out.*)

HUMFREY (*coming* R.C.).   Never heard of *champagne* . . . *ça me
fait rire* . . . (*With a high laugh.*)   Oh, la, la !   In Paris we drank
nothing else . . . the only drink for a gentleman.

PEPYS.   You were a pretty little choir-boy of Captain Cook's
when I last saw you, Mr. Humfrey—you have grown.   (*Turning* L.
to above table.)

HUMFREY.   *Ma foi!*   Yes . . . six years ago . . . I have learned
a lot since then.

PELLING.   Give us a taste of your learning then . . . will you
play this minuet of Lulli ?   (*Pointing to the music on the table.*)

(HUMFREY *moves to top of table.*)

HUMFREY (*glancing at it*).   That ?   *Ah bas! non* . . . that is
vieux jeu already.   (*Producing a cithern and roll of music from the
green bag.*)   I will give you a little thing of Lulli . . . *le dernier cri,*
a *minuet chanté exquis* written for the next play of M. Molière, " *Le
Bourgeois Gentilhomme.*"

(*Enter* BOY *with tankard.*)

The accompaniment is for cithern, lute, and flageolet.   *N'est ce pas,*
M. Pepys, you play the flageolet ?   *M. Cæsar m'a dit* . . . (*He
hands a part to* PEPYS, *another to* CÆSAR, *who has just received his
tankard of ale from the* BOY *who waits.*)

PEPYS.   I do my best.   (*He takes his flageolet from the table* L.)
A better drink than champagne, I wager, eh, Mr. Cæsar ?

(CÆSAR *goes on drinking.*)

CÆSAR (*giving his tankard to* BOY).   Best in the world, sir.

HUMFREY (*seating himself at the head of the table*).   Come, we are
ready.

(PEPYS *bridles a little, then sits beside him above the table.*)

Non, non, pas la . . . over there, the lute beside me.

[PELLING *sits in chair at the* L. *end of the table.* PEPYS *moves down.*
CÆSAR *takes his place with his lute.*)

And remember, *Monsieur le Flageolet, piáno, piáno, presque piánis-
simo.* I shall throw something at you if you drown the voice.

(PEPYS *rears slightly, but controls himself, lays his music before him,
leans same against the wine bottle, and puts on his green glasses.*)

Attention ! (*Rapping the table, then a single rap and they start the
accompaniment.* HUMFREY *sings. When the song is over:*) What
think you of that, Mr. Pepys ?
PEPYS.   A mighty sweet air.
PELLING.   Spring in it . . .
PEPYS.   But your Lulli uses harmonies of Italy.
CÆSAR.   You're in the right, sir.
HUMFREY.   *Ah non pardie ! Quelle bêtise* . . . he had **a** father
from Italy, *c'est vrai,*

(*The* BOY *enters* R.C.)

but it is French music, the best in the world.
BOY.   Sir, Mistress Pierce and Mistress Knepp are asking for
you.
PEPYS.   Bid them enter . . . and mighty glad they've come.
(*Rising.*)   Faith, here's a lady to sing you an English song will make
you change your tune, Mossoo Humfrey.   (*Goes* R. *to meet the ladies.*)
HUMFREY (*laughing*).   For a lady I will change anything, *pardie !*

(*The* BOY *shows in* MRS. PIERCE, *a handsome woman, very painted,
and* MRS. KNEPP, *a saucily attractive young woman.*)

PEPYS.   Welcome, my dears, my wife's from home, but I'm
heartily glad to see you.   (*Shaking hands with* MRS. PIERCE, *then
with* MRS. KNEPP, *who kisses him, and he her.*)
MRS. PIERCE.   Brute ! What have *I* done ?
MRS. KNEPP.   Missed the tide, i' faith.

(MRS. PIERCE *holds out her cheek. He kisses it reluctantly.*)

PEPYS (*softly*).   I feared to disturb the blush.
MRS. PIERCE (*pushing him*).   Monster, I hate you !
PEPYS (*taking one on each arm*).   Ladies, let me present Mr. Pel-
ham Humfrey, so fresh from Paris he can scarce speak English.
HUMFREY (C.).   *Mesdames . . . serviteur, serviteur.* (*A low bow
to each.*)

(*The Ladies curtsy.*)

MRS. KNEPP (*crossing* L. *to above table*).   Ave Cæsar ! (*To* CÆSAR.
She whispers.)

(CÆSAR *laughs and shakes his head.* MRS. KNEPP *sits in chair* L. *of table, offered her by* PELLING, *who continues talking to her.*)

MRS. PIERCE (*going* R.C.).   Pray, Mr. Humfrey, do the ladies wear panniers in Paris ?

HUMFREY.   *Mon Dieu, madame,* the pannier is as *démodé* as the fig-leaf—the maids who had them from their mistresses three years ago have cut them into saques a twelvemonth since.

PEPYS (*who has been listening, comes between* MRS. PIERCE *and* HUMFREY).   There is nothing good in England that hath not come from Paris and been so long on the way that it stinks of antiquity.

(MRS. PIERCE *sits on chest* R.)

Perish me ! (*Crossing* L. *above table.*)   Let's have one of our rotten English airs—Bab, sing us " Barbary Allen."

MRS. KNEPP.   Oh, Lud, no !

HUMFREY.   But that is not English, M. Pepys . . . it is Scotch !

(PEPYS *stares at him annoyed.* MRS. KNEPP *laughs.*)

Let me have a song *vrai* English.   You sing, M. Pepys, you compose —sing me a song of your own, and I accept the challenge.

MRS. KNEPP.   Yes, Sam, sing " Beauty Retire."

PELLING.   Ay, faith, " Beauty Retire " ! (*Crosses* L. *and sits on chest by* MRS. PIERCE.)

HUMFREY.   *Allons !* " Beauty Retire."

PEPYS.   You challenged me, I may choose my weapon. (*Going to cupboard.*)   I will sing " Gaze not on Swans." (*He takes out the parts, handing one to* CÆSAR, *another to* HUMFREY.)

HUMFREY.   *Eh bien,* " Gaze not on Swans " ;   *c'est la même chose,* and very good advice to young Ledas—— (*Takes up cithern and sits chair head of table.*)

PEPYS (*clears his throat*).   Are we ready ?

(*They begin the accompaniment, he sings, standing. During the first verse* HUMFREY *beats time impatiently with his foot, trying to quicken it. At the end of the first verse he becomes more impatient and calls out,* "Too slow, too slow ! "   PEPYS *controls his annoyance and starts the second verse, but is stopped by* HUMFREY.)

HUMFREY.   Charming ; but, *mon Dieu !* why make it a dirge ? Too slow, Mr. Pepys, too slow !

PEPYS.   Too slow !   But these are swans, sir !   Swans !

HUMFREY.   *N'importe* (*rises and puts cithern on stool*) . . . but your *tempo* is wrong ; it should be ta-ta-ta-tum, ta-ta-ta-ta. (*He hums the tune quickly.*)

PEPYS.   Those are geese, silly damned waddling geese. And i'gad, you seem to have spent a deal of your time in their company. (*He sits.*)

MRS. KNEPP (*patting his hand*).   Never mind him, Peepsey, it was mighty fine.

HUMFREY.   The English music—Oh, *mon Dieu*!   It is made of beer, pudding, fogs—one is buried under it.   But the French is alive, it sparkles—like champagne—like the ladies of France.

MRS. KNEPP.   Oh, I vow you are a toad!   (*Jumping up.*)   Am I made of beer and pudding and fogs . . .?

HUMFREY.   *Mais non, madame*, never, *mais non*—you are the exception that proves the rule.   (*Bowing to her.*)

(MRS. KNEPP *curtsies and sits again.*)

MRS. PIERCE.   Wretch!   Do you say that to my face!   (*Rising.*)

HUMFREY (*turning*).   My back was to your face, madame, or I could never have said it . . . you . . . you are the rule that proves the exception.   (*Bowing.*)

MRS. PIERCE (*curtsying, all smiles*).   Oh, sir, you overwhelm me. (*Coming* C.)   But indeed, Mr. Humfrey, there are some ladies I know—I name no names—who might learn from the French.

HUMFREY (*laughing*).   *Je crois bien, madame*, we have seen them in hundreds.

MRS. PIERCE.   Oh, in thousands, have we not?   (*Laughing, goes and sits on chest* R.)

PEPYS.   Ay, faith, learn to pinch their feet, distort their bodies, paint their faces, multiply their hair and grimace with all the affectations of an ape at a Christmas show.   The English woman is as God made her, egad, and beautiful, and better than all your flimsy foreign imitations that come to pieces in your hand.

HUMFREY (*laughing*).   *Mais c'est un drôle ce Pepys!*

(*The* BOY *hurries in* R.C.)

BOY.   The mistress is home, sir.

(*As* PEPYS *turns to meet her, all rise.*   MRS. PIERCE *goes down* R. PELLING *to below chest.*   MRS. PEPYS *sweeps in, cloaked and hooded and followed by her maid* LETTICE *carrying parcels and other wraps.* MRS. PEPYS, *who speaks with traces of a French accent, is a beautiful young woman of 29 and dressed with taste and richness.*)

MRS. PEPYS.   Lord!   we have company, so it seems . . .

PEPYS.   I' faith, for a little music.

MRS. PEPYS.   And Mistress Pierce and Mistress Knepp, too . . . I am honoured in my absence.   Good morrow to you, Pelling.

MRS. PIERCE.   We heard the playing, Mistress Pepys, as we came by, so could not forbear asking how you did.

MRS. PEPYS.   And wept, I dare swear, to find me away.   (*Throwing her hood and cloak to* LETTICE.)

PEPYS.   My treasure, let me present Mr. Pelham Humfrey . . . my wife, sir, an English beauty.

HUMFREY (*who has been eyeing her with satisfaction*). *Je suis ravi, madame, de faire votre connaissance.* (*With a very low bow as she curtsies.*) *Pardon,* I should have expressed my admiration in English. (*Kissing her hand.*)

MRS. PEPYS (*delighted*). *Oh! mais je comprend parfaitement, monsieur!*

HUMFREY. *Mais quel accent!* (*Turning to* PEPYS.) M. Pepys, I am vanquished—I ran a French rapier through your music, but you give me the *coup de grâce* with the beauty of your wife.

MRS. PEPYS. You have studied flattery in Paris, sir.

HUMFREY. And yet—how is it madame speaks French like a Parisian, and in her English, too, a *je ne sais quoi?*

MRS. PEPYS. My father is French.

HUMFREY. Ah ha! (*Triumphantly.*)

MRS. PEPYS. From my fourth year until just before I married, I lived in France.

HUMFREY. I knew it! Madame is French! (*He laughs.*) And Mr. Pepys is wrong again as usual.

PEPYS. Sir (*rising*), my wife is English by birth, speech, marriage and inclination—her father was an accident. (*Sitting again.*)

HUMFREY (*laughing*). A father is always an accident!—and sometimes a catastrophe. You are *vraie Parisienne, madame* . . . I knew it the moment I saw you . . . I felt it here. (*Laying his hand on his heart.*)

PEPYS (*rising—to* MRS. KNEPP). Lord! I could drown this puppy! (*Comes down* L. *of* MRS. KNEPP.)

MRS. KNEPP. Filthy creature! Faugh!

HUMFREY (*looking at his watch*). Six o'clock, *mon Dieu!* At half-past I am due at Whitehall. . . . *Je suis désolé, madame* . . . but His Majesty insists I sing him the Bergerette of Lulli . . . *allons, Cæsar!* (HUMFREY *puts cithern in bag, helped by* PEPYS. CÆSAR *picks up three sheets of music.*) Poor man, he will die if I come not, the music he hears is *horrible!* (*Kissing her hand.*) *Au revoir, chère madame.*

MRS. PEPYS. But I have not heard you sing—shall I not die? (PEPYS *hears this.*) Pray, Mr. Humfrey, sup with us to-night and sing after.

(PEPYS *turns again to* MRS. KNEPP.)

I dote on music, and Mr. Pepys loves it more than life, wife, or—who is it now, Samuel?

(PEPYS *frowns.*)

HUMFREY. *Enchanté, madame.*

PEPYS (*moving to* L.C.) To-night does not suit me, i' faith. . . . I shall be late to-night . . . much business at the office—for the launching of a new ship, ay (*going down* L.), and other matters.

(*All rise.*)

MRS. PEPYS. Pish! then we can sup late. (*To* HUMFREY.) Come at nine, and if Mr. Pepys be late you can talk French to me till he come.

HUMFREY. *Enchanté.* (*Kissing her hand.*) *À neuf heures alors.* (*Bowing to the others.*) M. *Pepys . . . monsieur, mesdames!* *Allons, Cæsar!* The King is waiting for me. (*He goes out, followed by* CÆSAR.)

(MR. PEPYS *glares furiously at his wife till* HUMFREY *is gone.*)

PEPYS (*crossing* C., *controlling his rage*). Supper at nine, i'gad! Mighty pleasant, ha, ha! Then Mistress Pierce and Mistress Knepp shall sup with us, too.

(MRS. PEPYS *sits on stool in front of table.*)

Pelling is already bidden and hath bestowed a hare. The frog's music shall not have all his own way, and we'll make a merry night of it. What say you, ladies?

(MRS. PEPYS *glares at him.*)

MRS. KNEPP. Yes—quick! (*Moving to* C. *above table.*)
MRS. PIERCE (*rising*). Enchanted—if Mistress Pepys will not be too tired.
MRS. PEPYS (*forcing a smile*). Oh, no! I am not easily tired. (*Rising.*) But Mistress Knepp will be at the Playhouse?
MRS. KNEPP. I don't play; 'tis that silly piece "Hamlet."
MRS. PIERCE. Well, let's away. Mr. Pelling, will you squire us to our lodgings? Till nine, Mistress Pepys. (*Curtsying.*)
MRS. KNEPP. Till nine. (*Curtsies.*)
MRS. PEPYS. Yes, *nine.* (*Curtsies.*)

(MRS. PIERCE *goes out with* PEPYS. MRS. KNEPP *follows with* PELLING. *A loud laugh from* MRS. PIERCE.)

MRS. PEPYS. Hussies!

(*Street door is heard to bang.*)

(MRS. PEPYS *flings herself into the chair* R. *of table and sits tapping her foot.*)

(PEPYS *returns, coming towards* MRS. PEPYS.)

PEPYS. Lord! What a pickle you put me in asking that fellow——
MRS. PEPYS. Fellow!
PEPYS. An English pup, French polished . . . jabbering and aping with his silly vanity till I nearly spewed. (*Goes down* R.)
MRS. PEPYS. Ouf! Filthy! *He* did not talk foul like that.
PEPYS. No; he hasn't the sense to know his own language.

MRS. PEPYS. He knows his manners.

PEPYS. Coxcomb manners, rude, lewd, saucy manners, and you like 'em! (*Coming up to* MRS. PEPYS.)

MRS. PEPYS. I confess I found him mighty pleasant.

PEPYS. No doubt, ma'am, no doubt. His leering at you——

MRS. PEPYS. He didn't leer at me.

PEPYS. Zoons, woman, I saw him do it—like that. (*He sticks his face at her with his eyes starting out of his head.*)

(MRS. PEPYS *bursts out laughing.*)

MRS. PEPYS. Had he made faces like that I should have died o' laughing—ha! ha! ha!

PEPYS. Ha! ha! ha! mighty funny, by the Lord, mighty funny with your husband looking on, woman.

MRS. PEPYS. 'Tis very vulgar to call your wife a woman.

PEPYS. You were woman to him, I warrant . . . kissing your hand, and squeezing it too, I'll be sworn——

MRS. PEPYS (*springing up*). 'Tis a lie!

PEPYS. Pressing it and mumbling it with his lips——

MRS. PEPYS. 'Tis your own wicked mind makes you think thus. He treated me with perfect respect (*moving to* L.), and 'tis a pleasant change to be with a man who talks civil. (*Turning to* PEPYS.) Besides, I asked him for your sake.

PEPYS. For my sake!

MRS. PEPYS (*crossing to* C.). Because he sings and plays, and *you* are mad for music.

PEPYS. For my sake! A jackanapes, who laughed in my face when I sang, mocked our music, and allows no one to know anything but himself—(C.) and then, forsooth, you ask him to sup with us.

MRS. PEPYS. And you ask the Pierce woman and the Knepp woman to sup, and you know I can't abide them.

PEPYS. 'Twas to even you for the Frenchman—and 'tis very vulgar to call people woman.

MRS. PEPYS. No—not when the women are vulgar people!

(PEPYS *turns away.*)

And you vowed to me, and gave it me under your hand, you would never see 'em again while you lived.

PEPYS (*turning to her*). And I kept my vow. Lord (*turning away*), woman, is it my fault they came when you were out to ask how you did? (*Crossing down* R.)

MRS. PEPYS. Ask how I did! Ha! ha! . . . much they care. Did they ever come while I was home? No, not in six months and more. (*Coming* C.) I begin to think I can't trust you out of my sight. And all this business at the office, taking you abroad by night . . . humph!

PEPYS (*coming to her*). The King's business is done by night as well as by day.

Mrs. Pepys. Faith, I don't doubt that. (*He turns up stage.*)
What is this business to-night?

Pepys (*coming down to her*). I told you . . . for the launching
of a new ship.

Mrs. Pepys. They don't launch ships by night.

Pepys. No—nor they don't launch ships in the office neither.
But I must be there for preparations . . . tallies to see to—for
guns . . . masts . . . sails . . . muster-roll . . . and a hundred
things, that not a day be lost in her commissioning.

Mrs. Pepys (*unimpressed*). What is the name of the ship?

Pepys. *The Great Beare.*

Mrs. Pepys. Well, I'll believe you this time.

Pepys. 'Tis mighty good of you! (*Crossing down* R.)

Mrs. Pepys. But if ever I find that *The Great Beare* sails in
petticoats and a silken bodice—I'll scratch her eyes out. (*Moving
towards him.*)

(Pepys *cannot help laughing.*)

Pepys. Egad, you may, and welcome! (*Going* L. *to her and
putting his arms round her.*) Come, wife, don't be vexed . . . let's
be friends and give up fighting.

Mrs. Pepys. Well, but who began it?

Pepys. No, no, let's not talk of who began it, or we'll begin
again. I began it, but you provoked me to it.

Mrs. Pepys. Oh, but it was you who—— (*She draws away
from him.*)

Pepys (*following her up*). Yes, yes . . . (*kissing her*)—it was I
who angered you to provoke me to begin it, and so on back to
the first beginning, which was when we fell from grace and
got married. (*He coaxes her round to him, kissing her.*) So we're
friends.

Mrs. Pepys. And you don't prefer that slut Knepp to me?

Pepys. I don't care if I never see the jade again, and I won't if
I can help it.

(Mrs. Pepys *kisses him.*)

Mrs. Pepys. There! And I may have that green taffety gown
with silver lacing, above my allowance? . . .

(Pepys *draws away, annoyed.*)

You said I might——

Pepys. No such thing. I said I *might* give it you if . . .

Mrs. Pepys. Ay, faith! (*Turning away to* L.) 'Tis little enough
your kisses are worth . . .

Pepys (*coming to her*). Well, well . . . yes, yes, you shall have
it. I did mean you should have it, but not yet.

Mrs. Pepys. Then we're friends. (*She kisses him and runs to the foot of the stairs.*) And I may have one of the new lace scarves to wear with it ?

PEPYS (C.). No, no !

MRS. PEPYS. Yes, yes !

PEPYS. Faith, no ! Gad, would you ruin me !

MRS. PEPYS. Oh, please say yes !

PEPYS. Well, some day—I'll think about it.

MRS. PEPYS (*she blows him a kiss, runs upstairs, then turns at the top*). Well, promise me you'll never look that odious Pierce woman in the face again after to-night.

PEPYS. I swear it ! I'gad, no one will ever look her in the face again without she strips two coats of paint off.

(MRS. PEPYS *runs laughing to the door of her room, then leaning over the gallery.*)

MRS. PEPYS. And when do you take me to Unthankes for the gown ?

PEPYS. Soon.

MRS. PEPYS. To-morrow?

PEPYS. Lord ! Yes . . . to-morrow . . . to-morrow. (*Sitting in chair at head of table.*)

(MRS. PEPYS *blows him a kiss and goes into her room. The bedroom door bangs. He heaves a great sigh of relief.*)

Peace is mighty pleasant . . . at any price. (*He looks at his watch.*) Seven . . . in half an hour I must be going. (*Singing to himself " Beauty Retire," he rises and goes to the cupboard L. and begins looking through sheets of music, then stops and calls.*) Jacke ! Boy ! Jacke ! (*He resumes his search, finally selects a sheet, finishes he phrase, looking at it, folds it and puts it in his pocket.*)

(JACKE *enters up* R.)

Come hither, Jacke.

(*The* BOY *comes down.*)

Fetch my satchel and wait for me by the door. . . . I am going to the office . . . you shall carry it there. When I am in, you need not wait ; come home. And if any (*looking up at bedroom door*) should ask you where I be, you will know . . . at the Navy Office . . . so you can speak the truth. And . . . here is twelvepence for you, and a good lad. (*He gives him twelve pennies, pats him on the back.*)

(*The* BOY *exits up* R.)

(PEPYS *looks round for his flageolet, sees it on the table, puts it in his pocket.*)

(LETTICE *enters from above and is going downstairs.*)

Come here to me, girl.

LETTICE.   What be your pleasure, zur ?

PEPYS.   Faith, some of it, looking at you, Lettice.

LETTICE (*giggling and wriggling*).   Oh, zur !

PEPYS (*singing softly and going towards her*).
      " The prettiest gurl that e'er I saw-aw-aw
      Was zucking zyder thro' a straw-aw-aw."

LETTICE (*wriggling*).   Oh, do 'ee leave me alone, maister.

PEPYS.   The devil of it is, I can't, Lettice. (*Putting his arm round her, which she eludes by crossing* L.)   Have you done your singing exercise to-day ?

LETTICE.   No, zur.

PEPYS (*shaking his finger*).   Bad girl.   Did I not make you promise never to miss a single day ?

LETTICE.   Oh, zur, how could I to-day ?   Zeeing I be all day in the coach . . . an' bevore I go all the linen to count.

PEPYS.   Well, don't forget 'em before you go to bed.

LETTICE.   No, maister.

PEPYS.   For your voice is soft as cream, and if you practise you will sing like a bird. (*Lifting her chin.*)   Do you know that ?

LETTICE.   'Ee do zay zo.

PEPYS.   And 'tis true. Come, let me hear it. (*Singing.*)   Do—re—mi—fa—so—la—si—do.

LETTICE (*singing*).   Do—re—mi—fa—so—la—si—do.

PEPYS.   Mighty pretty !   But breathe deeply . . . fill that lovely breast. And keep the lips apart . . . for i'gad, when you keep 'em together I can't resist 'em. (*He bends forward and kisses her on the lips.*)

(*A second earlier* MRS. PEPYS, *in petticoats and dressing-jacket, has come from their room and sees it from the gallery.*)

MRS. PEPYS (*with a cry of fury*).   Jemini !

(PEPYS *hears her, and without turning whips his flageolet out of his pocket. He blows a long note.*)

PEPYS.   Now sing that note.

(LETTICE, *pulled together by his firmness, sings the note loud and long, and by the time* MRS. PEPYS *arrives at the foot of the stairs* LETTICE *is still holding the note, and* PEPYS, *with the flageolet to his lips, bent forward, staring down her throat.*)

Head up—chest full—mouth well open.

MRS. PEPYS.   Samuel !

PEPYS (*without moving*).   Yes, my love—tongue well down . . that's better !

        (LETTICE *finishes the note.*)

Much better . . . mighty good this time.

Mrs. Pepys. Samuel! What are you doing?

Pepys (*without turning*). Teaching a lesson to the girl, my dear. Forget not what I showed you, and do the exercise six times before bed. Run along now, that's a good girl. (*Crosses to table and puts down the flageolet and puts on his glasses.*)

(Lettice *drops a curtsy and hurries out* R.)

Mrs. Pepys *stares at her speechless as she goes by.*)

Mrs. Pepys. You were kissing her!

Pepys (*turning and coming* c.). Kissing her! Are you mad?

Mrs. Pepys. I saw you.

Pepys. I'gad, you must be, if you saw that.

Mrs. Pepys. Serpent! Did I not see you kiss her with my own eyes from up there?

Pepys. No, viper, you did not!

Mrs. Pepys. I saw you bent forward with your head close up against hers and you kissed her.

Pepys. You saw me bent forward with my head close up against hers, and I looking into her mouth and down her throat to make sure she kept her tongue in place and governed her voice according to the proper methods of instructing pupils in the art of song.

Mrs. Pepys. Monstrous impudence! . . . Am I not to believe my own eyes?

Pepys. Your eyes deceived you, basely, and lied with the same effrontery as your tongue.

Mrs. Pepys (*sullenly*). I know you were kissing her.

Pepys. And I know I was teaching her to sing proper. (*Moving* L. *and sitting in chair at the head of the table.*)

Mrs. Pepys. Very like indeed! . . . As if I hadn't seen you looking at her before now.

Pepys. Lord! 'Tis enough to make one mad! May a man not look at the maids in his own house, ma'am?

Mrs. Pepys. With that eye . . . with that rogue's eye——

Pepys. Or would you like to keep me blindfold at home (*removing his glasses*), and lead me about, and feed me with a spoon forsooth?

Mrs. Pepys. That eye—that I have watched these five years, with Mistress Daniel, and Betty Turner, and Pierce and Knepp, and Jane and Deb Willett and——

Pepys (*rising*). And—and every woman in London and the country round, who ever came within five feet of me. S'life! If 'tis the ancient history lecture again, I know it by heart! (*Goes down* L.)

Mrs. Pepys. Heart! (c.) Ay, a rotten heart with holes made in it by women, till it's no better than a sieve.

PEPYS (*moving up to her*). And your mind's a warren, woman, with jealousy and imagination breeding like rabbits and trying to father all the progeny on me. (*Looking at his watch.*) But I disown the bastards . . . (*crossing quickly to the foot of the stairs*) you can nurse 'em yourself . . . I've got other work to do.

MRS. PEPYS. Why do you look at your watch ?

PEPYS. Because . . . (*Stops and turns to her.*)

MRS. PEPYS. Because—(*she bursts into a loud laugh*)—you're afraid you may miss the ship . . . she may miss the tide . . . she may be launched without you . . . she may be gone ! Ha ! ha ! ha ! Ha ! ha !

(*He sticks his fingers to his ears and goes up the stairs.*)

There shall be no more pretty maids ! . . . I'll look out a new set . . . they shall be thin . . . and toothless . . . and squint . . . and pock-marked from head to foot if I can find 'em !

(*He goes into their room, banging the door.*)

(*She becomes quieter at once, turning away and sitting in the chair at the R. end of the table, drumming her fingers on it and thinking what to do. She picks up the sheet of music before her, glances at it, and throws it aside, then suddenly her attention is caught by the written paper which lay under it. She stares at it a moment, then picks it up and reads.*)

"Willow House . . . North Side . . . Gray's Inn Fields." (*She looks up with a puzzled expression, then at the door where PEPYS went out, then springing up folds the paper and puts it in her dress and goes quickly towards the stairs, then stops, changes her mind, goes up to the back and calls softly.*) Jacke ! Jacke !

(*The BOY comes on, carrying PEPYS' satchel.*)

(*She takes him by the arm down stage C.*) Listen to me, Jacke. You're a good boy, aren't you ?

BOY. Yes, mistress.

MRS. PEPYS. And you're truthful ?

BOY. Yes, mistress.

MRS. PEPYS. And you've got to do something for me.

BOY. Yes, mistress.

MRS. PEPYS. When you go out with the master—do you know where Mrs. Pierce lodges ?

BOY. Yes, mistress.

MRS. PEPYS. And Mistress Knepp ?

BOY. Yes, mistress.

MRS. PEPYS. Well, when you go out with the master, come straight back and tell me where he is.

BOY. Yes, mistress.

MRS. PEPYS. And (*she feels in a pocket in corsage*) here is twelvepence for you, and a good boy. (*She gives him the coin and pats him on the head.*)

(*He turns to go, putting satchel on chest* R.)

Wait . . . do you know who lodges at Willow House . . . North Side . . . Gray's Inn Fields ?

BOY (*scratches his head, then shakes it slowly*). I've never been *there* !

MRS. PEPYS (*softly, as* PEPYS *enters above*). Get along.

(*Exit* JACKE *up* R.)

(PEPYS *comes down the stairs. He has changed the upper half of his attire for a flowered tabby vest and coloured camelot tunique with gold lace at the cuffs. He wears a new black hat at the back of his head.* MRS. PEPYS *watches him come down with a bitter smile.*)

Oh ho ! we are very *fine* to-night, i' faith . . . our new flowered tabby vest put on . . . and our coloured coat as well, mighty fine, forsooth !

(PEPYS *goes past her with his mouth tightly shut, and going to the table, lays his stick on it and begins searching among the sheets of music, lifting each in turn.*)

And our best black hat . . . and worn in the Monmouth cock, too ! . . . I vow and swear, Mr. Pepys, you look a picture . . . you should be painted so, faith, you should.

(PEPYS *not finding what he seeks, looks on the floor.*)

What are you seeking for ? Eh ? . . . Do you hear me ? . . . What ? What is it ? What have you lost ?

(*He does not answer, but goes to the cupboard and looks there.*)

(*At head of table.*) And pray what is the meaning of all this finery ? Shall I tell you ? 'Tis in honour of the ship . . . ay, that's it, for a ship's a she ; and we're mighty gallant ; so we put on all our best clothes to go to the office by night . . . (*crossing* R.C.) out of compliment to *The Great Beare* ! (*She laughs hysterically.*)

(PEPYS *returns to the table, gathers up the music and puts it in the cupboard.*)

But if I were you I should have worn my black . . . you keep your dignity in black . . . your coloured coat and vest make you look ridiculous . . . it's hideous, monstrous ! (*Returning to head of table.*) Do you know what you look like ? . . . I'll tell you . . . like a great swelling turkey cock two weeks before Christmas. . . . Yes ! Just—just before it gets its throat cut !

(PEPYS *has returned to the table, picks up the flageolet and puts it in his pocket.*)

So, you take *that* with you! Why? Do you play tunes in the office, eh? Why don't you answer me . . . can't you hear me talking? . . . Why don't you answer?

(PEPYS, *who has gone up to the back, gives a sharp whistle, then picks up his stick from the table.*)

Answer . . . answer . . . answer . . . speak, answer me, I say!

(*The* BOY *comes on.* PEPYS *points to the satchel, which the* BOY *picks up, then points to the door with his stick. The* BOY *goes, and with a look round the room,* PEPYS *follows.*)

You won't answer . . . I'll tell you why . . . you're so full of lies that they'd choke you if you opened your mouth. Going to the office . . . liar! Launching a ship . . . liar! liar! But wait, wait . . . I'll be even with you . . . you wait, you black-hearted villain . . . I'll sink your *Great Beare*!

(*The street door bangs.*)

Dog! (*For a moment she stands silent, panting, then runs down, calling.*) Lettice! Lettice! Lettice! (*Through the door* R. *front.*) Lettice! I'm going out!

(*She runs up the stairs, followed a moment later by* LETTICE.)

Quick! I'm going out! . . . My new gown . . . my gold shoes . . . my cloak . . . my hood . . . I'm going out . . . I'm going out.

(*She goes into her room, banging the door in* LETTICE'S *face.*)

CURTAIN.

ACT II

SCENE.—MRS. KNIGHT'S *Lodging in Gray's Inn Fields. High curtained windows at the back. Entrance from the ante-room, half-way down on the* R. *and facing the audience. Entrance to the bedroom, similarly half-way down on the* L. *and facing the audience. The room is luxuriously furnished. A harpsichord* L.C., *a music-stand, and other musical instruments. Against the wall* R., *just above the angle of the door, an Italian table with a mirror above it and pots of cosmetics, etc., on it. A couch, chairs, etc., and below the harpsichord a large Italian Renaissance marriage chest. A few paintings on the walls, also a small painting of Charles II above the mantelpiece* R.

(MRS. KNIGHT'S *voice is heard singing before the* CURTAIN *rises, when she is discovered seated at the harpsichord, strumming and singing snatches of song.* JULIA *is standing behind her dressing her hair.*)

JULIA. You are too reckless, madam, and I say it again—treading mean streets and filthy lanes and crooked alleys, without ever a man . . . and it isn't the first time I've said it, and——

MRS. KNIGHT. And it won't be the last, Julia. (*She sings a few bars of another song, then looks for another.*)

(JULIA *curling and dressing her hair.*)

JULIA (*standing back and looking at the effect*). No, it wouldn't surprise *me* to hear you'd had your head hacked off and the other half plumped in the Thames like the chandler's daughter at Wapping . . . that's what I say. (*Again dressing her hair.*) Shall I pin these curls higher ?

MRS. KNIGHT. Oh, leave 'em as they are.

JULIA (*stepping back again*). No, or *beaten* to death and thrown on a dungheap, with every bone broken, like the pious lady at Islington . . . no, indeed ! . . . or the poor washerwoman of Woolwich, carved in fine slices and laid in her own tub.

MRS. KNIGHT. O gad, I cannot endure this meaty conversation. . . . Be quiet, child, or I'll marry you to a butcher next Tuesday, and you shall watch him carve joints and break bones for the rest of your life. Where do you get this thirst for blood ?

JULIA. A body must have **something** lively to talk of.

MRS. KNIGHT. Then talk of men, not of mangled meat.

(JULIA *crosses to dressing-table and tidies up.*)

(Mrs. Knight *sings several bars of another song.*)

Julia (*turns to* Mrs. Knight). I doubt not your head's agog with this Pepys person.

Mrs. Knight. Person! You jade . . . where should I be *but* for Mr. Pepys . . . in your Thames or your washerwoman's tub maybe.

Julia. Oh! It fair makes me go goosey all over! (*With a final touch to* Mrs. Knight's *hair.*) There, that's an elegant head. But faith, he had a gamesome eye . . . a rogue with the women, if ever *I* saw one!

Mrs. Knight (*laughing*). What I dote on in a man is courage . . . to think of him near beating the life out of that great hulking villain, crimine!

Julia. Ay, I would I had seen that!

Mrs. Knight. Faith, so would I . . . but I swooned, till I found myself in my saviour's arms. (*Rising and laughing.*) O gad! I swear I am as great a beast for blood as you, Julia, for I think to be by and see men fight for one is near the best thing in life. (*At mirror over table R.*)

Julia. Ay, madam, very near it. (*Takes hare's foot from harpsichord and gives to* Mrs. Knight—*then back for glass tray which she gives to her.*)

Mrs. Knight. O Lard! What a face for a welcome! . . . gaunt and chalky, like Dover cliff on a wet morning. . . . I vow I must redden a trifle.

Julia (L. *of chair by dressing-table*). The least touch, madam . . . pale and languid is more becoming you . . . it gives you that dying look.

Mrs. Knight. Pish, child!

Julia. But sure you ain't *serious* on this Mr. Pepys——

Mrs. Knight. Save me from ever being serious.

Julia. What is he?

Mrs. Knight. Mighty civil and pleasant.

Julia. And what could *he* give you? . . .

Mrs. Knight. He gave me all I have . . . I shouldn't be here if he hadn't been there.

Julia. I wouldn't throw myself away if my Lord Codbury was dying for me.

Mrs. Knight. He's too old to do anything *but* die for me.

Julia. He's rich.

Mrs. Knight. He's eighty. Filthy fellow . . . I had my *fill* of ruins in Rome——

Julia. And young Sir Hercules Wrotford——

Mrs. Knight. Smells all horses and tobacco. . . . Foh!

Julia (*looking at picture of Charles*). Troth, and who knows what day old Rowley mayn't be here again. (*Goes to harpsichord and tidies music.*)

MRS. KNIGHT (*throwing down the hare's foot*). Don't speak of him, girl! (*Going down* R. *in front of fireplace.*) 'Tis finished. . . . We shan't see him again, save in a side box.

JULIA (*nodding sagely*). I put my shift on wrong side out this morning.

MRS. KNIGHT (*still looking at picture*). The Castlemaine and that slut Nelly have got him, each an ear . . . pull devil, pull baker, and God save the King. (*Crossing round to foot of couch and sitting on it.*) Draw the curtains, child.

JULIA (*drawing them at windows* R., *then* L.). Many a hare has bolted between two hounds.

MRS. KNIGHT. They can keep him, the whole pack of them. I'm not minded to be harem-hanger-on to anyone.

(*Knocking heard on the door below.*)

If that be Mr. Pepys, bring him up . . . if not, I am ill or out, whatever lie comes first. Run, girl.

(JULIA *hurries out by* R., *closing the door.* MRS. KNIGHT *goes to the mirror, humming to herself, twists a curl on her front, then looks round the room; decides on the harpsichord, sits, plays a few bars, then changing her mind, springs up, goes to the mirror, wipes the red off her cheeks, powders, and snatching a book from the dressing-table, arranges herself " à la malade " on the couch* R., *her head propped on cushions and the book held half-closed on her breast.*)

JULIA (*holding the door wide*). Mr. Pepys, madam.

(PEPYS, *carrying hat and stick, enters with a nervous smile.*)

MRS. KNIGHT. Oh, Mr. Pepys, have you come?

PEPYS. Have I flown, madam . . . did you think I should fail? But do not tell me you are ill?

MRS. KNIGHT (*languidly*). But so so . . .

PEPYS. I am mighty sorry to hear it.

MRS. KNIGHT (*to* JULIA). That will do, child.

(JULIA *goes out, closing door.*)

Ay, faith, but so so . . . and were it not for you I might have been——

PEPYS. Perish the thought!

(*She extends a languid hand, which he kisses.*)

(*Taking a step back.*) But I trust my presence does not——

MRS. KNIGHT. Oh, no! I think it does me good . . . you are so vital, so brave . . . you give me courage to face life.

(PEPYS *bows.*)

Pray lay aside your hat and sit by me.

(PEPYS *lays hat and stick on the harpsichord and draws the music stool to* L. *of couch.*)

PEPYS. Faith, and mighty gladly. I did hurry so out of fear to be late, and not for the world would I have missed a minute of this wonderful night. (*Sitting.*) So !

MRS. KNIGHT. I think I feel better already.

PEPYS. When I look on you, egad, it puts me in a rage . . . ay, that I did not beat the ruffian to death.

MRS. KNIGHT (*closing her eyes*). Do not name him. I swooned again when I came home, and here I have lain ever since . . . trying to read.

PEPYS. Faith, then *I'll* read to you. I read mighty well . . . at home o' nights I read aloud to my . . . self.

MRS. KNIGHT. O Lard, no ! 'Tis a foolish book.

PEPYS. How is it called ?

MRS. KNIGHT. I have forgot . . . devil take it. (*Throwing book into the fireplace.*) There ! talk to me . . . tell me, do I not look frightfully . . . white . . . and drawn . . . with sunken eyes ?

PEPYS. Faith, I'll tell you . . . (*Moves stool nearer couch, then bending forward.*) You look divine, like a goddess in white marble . . . pale . . . and languid . . . and that dying look in your eyes . . . I swear I might swoon by mere gazing in 'em.

MRS. KNIGHT. Tell me more.

PEPYS. Would you have me swoon ? (*Taking her hand.*)

MRS. KNIGHT. No, for I might swoon with you, and three swoons a day is beyond my allowance. (*Drawing her hand away.*) And so for near two years you have been waiting to hear me sing ?

PEPYS. Egad, had I but seen your face, I had not waited two days, I had followed you——

MRS. KNIGHT. To Italy ?

PEPYS. To the world's end.

MRS. KNIGHT. How you must love music !

PEPYS. Indeed, indeed. And I think music and love are of like nature. I remember the first time I heard wind music . . . it was so sweet that it did wrap up my soul so that it made me really sick, just as I have been when in love . . . and I remained all night, transported.

MRS. KNIGHT. You *should* have followed me to Italy. The beauty of it ! . . . you would have lived in transport. Music . . . marble . . . the nights of stars ! Florence with the sound of strings streaming through the Loggia windows into the dark . . . the fountain's murmur in the garden below. Rome . . . St. Peter's . . . where the boys' voices climbed and climbed till they seemed to break upon the dome in sparkles of sound. A sea of music beating at the gates of heaven. Ob, you *should* have followed me to Italy !

PEPYS (*rising*). It would have made me mad ! (*Moving away to* c.) I' faith beauty does that with me . . . like wine in the head.

I climb up out of myself . . . I am another man. When I look
at your beauty . . . When I listen to your voice telling of wonderful things, (*returning and bending over and trying to take her hand*)
I feel . . .

MRS. KNIGHT (*rising on* R. *of the couch and eluding him*). You
forget you are in London where the streets are mud, not marble, and
people must be sane.

PEPYS. Impossible in your presence . . .

(*She curtsies, laughing.*)

But Italy has followed you here . . . your furniture ; your paintings—(*looking round*)—sure all these are of Italy ? (*Crossing to* L.
above chest.)

MRS. KNIGHT. Faith, I brought away all the wonders I could
beg, borrow, or buy. (*Pointing to picture* L.) That is by Caligari
the Veronese.

PEPYS. The splendour of Venice . . . mighty fine !

MRS. KNIGHT. This chest, Zacchiotto painted for me in Parma.
The Venus is Correggio's. (*Pointing* C.)

PEPYS (*coming* C.). Divine flesh tints truly. Humph ! And
what of that ? (*Pointing to the portrait over the mantelshelf.*)

MRS. KNIGHT. What ?

PEPYS (*crossing* R. *to fireplace*). Above the fireplace . . . that
portrait ?

MRS. KNIGHT. That is the King.

PEPYS. Egad I know that . . . but did that come from Italy ?

MRS. KNIGHT. Of course not. It was painted by Hales.

PEPYS. You bought it of him ?

MRS. KNIGHT. Why ! How ill-humoured you are of a sudden !
. . . It was given me . . . by His Majesty . . . the first time I
sang at Whitehall.

PEPYS (*looking at picture of Charles*). I like it not. The lips are
too full—a loose mouth . . . malicious eyes, and the nose obscene.

MRS. KNIGHT. Fie ! Mr. Pepys . . . treason !

PEPYS. Devil a bit, 'tis ill done. I know the King better (*turning to* MRS. KNIGHT), and he would give you a better portrait of me.

MRS. KNIGHT. Let me have it.

PEPYS (*crossing* L.). Take it from *him*, madam, take it from
him, a companion picture to the other.

MRS. KNIGHT. I never see him now.

PEPYS. Never ?

(*She sits looking at herself in the glass.*)

MRS. KNIGHT. Not these two years and more.

PEPYS (*delighted*). Faith if that's so, I'll give it you myself !
(*Coming up to her.*) Though I say it not for boastfulness, nor vain-
glory . . . but 'tis the truth. 'Twas after my speech in the House,
my defence of the Navy Commission . . . four hours by the clock

I spoke, and you might have heard a pin drop. The King said to me—with his own lips, mind you—" Mr. Pepys, I am very glad of your success yesterday."

MRS. KNIGHT. With his own lips ! (*Suppressing a smile.*)

PEPYS. Ay, but that was not all. Prodgers of the bedchamber swore to me, before witnesses too, the King said *I* might teach the Solicitor-General. And more, Mr. Montagu told the King *I* was another Cicero . . . Cicero, think of that . . . and His Majesty said " Ha ! "

MRS. KNIGHT. He said " Ha ! "

PEPYS. " Ha ! " To be sure, I say not these things of myself, I but say what was said, so you may know in what opinion His Majesty holds me.

MRS. KNIGHT. In my opinion my Cicero has a most persuasive tongue.

PEPYS (*bending over her chair*). Faith if my goddess would but listen, her Cicero could say such things to her . . . such sweet things as might persuade . . .

MRS. KNIGHT. Hush ! (*Putting the hare's foot with which she was about to rouge her cheeks against his lips.*)

PEPYS. 'Tis a hare's foot, egad ! (*Snatching it from her with his* R. *hand.*) This is no good ! (*Moving down a little.*)

MRS. KNIGHT. No good ?

PEPYS. It lacks the joint to it——

MRS. KNIGHT. The joint ?

PEPYS. If you would be safe against colic and rumblings within, your hare's foot must have the joint to it—like mine ! (*Producing his and holding one in each hand.*)

MRS. KNIGHT. Colic, rumblings, fie ! What beastly talk is this ?

PEPYS. Why ! (*Going back to* MRS. KNIGHT.) Do you not carry the hare's foot against colic ?

MRS. KNIGHT. The Lord forbid ! (*She laughs. Taking her hare's foot from him and raising it to her cheek.*) 'Tis to bring a blush to my cheek when my face is too pale.

PEPYS (*seizing her* L. *wrist with his* R. *hand*). No, faith, I forbid the blush, you shall not blush till I make you. You are pale, 'tis the beauty of you. The Bible forbids us to paint the lily . . . and I cannot abide a woman who paints. If the lily were not pale the butterfly would not light on it . . .

MRS. KNIGHT (*laughing*). You are breaking my arm, O ponderous butterfly !

PEPYS (*stepping back*). Egad, you are i' the right. I am no butterfly. I am the bee that goes straight for the honey. . . . (*He bends down to kiss her lips. She eludes him.*)

MRS. KNIGHT. And from your buzz a very daring insect I perceive. (*Crossing to the harpsichord below couch.*) I thought you came to hear me sing, not to teach me botany.

PEPYS. Ay, that is so—sing to me, soothe me, for your slave is getting out of hand. (*Replaces stool to harpsichord.*)

MRS. KNIGHT. Where is the new song you promised? . . . how was it called? . . . "Beauty Retire."

PEPYS. 'Tis here, and another I have writ called "Gaze not on Swans." Faith, had you not asked I had not dared bring them forth. (*Taking the MS. from his pocket.*)

MRS. KNIGHT. Let me see, "Beauty Retire." (*She hums a few bars.*) Oh, but this goes rarely.

PEPYS. Many indeed have liked it . . .

MRS. KNIGHT. Indeed.

PEPYS. It seems it is a fine song. Come, and I will give you the obligato on my flageolet. (*Producing his flageolet he moves to above harpsichord.*)

(MRS. KNIGHT *sings.* PEPYS *playing the flageolet.*)

SONG : "Beauty Retire."

MRS. KNIGHT.

Beauty retire, thou dost my pity move,
Believe my pity and then trust my love,
At first I thought her by our prophet sent
As a reward for valour's toils,
More worth than all my Father's spoils,
But now she is become my punishment ;
But thou art just, O pow'r divine,
With new and painful arts of studied war,
I break the hearts of half the world
And she breaks mine.

PEPYS (*when the song is over*). Ah ! I never heard singing the like of that and I have heard many. I cannot believe I wrote it.

MRS. KNIGHT. Oh, but Mr. Pepys, it *is* fine. When shall I come to the end of your gifts ! . . . A great orator . . . a great musician . . . a great fighter . . .

PEPYS. Faith, and you haven't touched on the best of them yet.

MRS. KNIGHT. And which is that ?

PEPYS. A great lover. (*Laying his flageolet on the harpsichord and bending towards her.*)

MRS. KNIGHT (*rising and stepping back to head of couch*). Nay, that were too many for one day . . . I might be afraid . . . I might have to follow the advice of your song.

PEPYS. The advice ?

MRS. KNIGHT. Beauty retire ! (*Crossing L.C. to below chest.*)

PEPYS. Retire—and let me follow. (*Coming down C.*)

MRS. KNIGHT. Nay, I don't trust you. I shall stand my ground

—(*she sits on the marriage chest*)—and talk to the great fighter, my hero to whom I have not given half the thanks——

PEPYS (R.C.).   Pooh, I am no hero——

MRS. KNIGHT.   Modest as well!

PEPYS.   'Tis the bare truth.   I love not fighting.

MRS. KNIGHT (*laughing*).   Oh, hear him!   He loves not fighting! When I came from my swoon your eyes were blazing.

PEPYS.   Blazing i' faith, ay, ha! ha! ha!

MRS. KNIGHT.   Your breath panting.

PEPYS.   Ha! ha! ha! ay, marry that was so.

MRS. KNIGHT.   Your limbs shaking with the lust of fight.

PEPYS.   Aye, quaking—shaking—egad, so 'twas!   For you I would have fought an army.   But, faith, the part of fighting I like best is when 'tis all over.   (*Sitting beside her.*)   When the victor comes to the fair and she gives him her hand to kiss.   (*He takes her hand and kisses it.*)   And lets him look into her eyes and see the promise of her lips.   (*He looks into her eyes.*)

MRS. KNIGHT (*turning away her head*).   No, no, not yet.

(PEPYS *kisses her hand violently.*)

Nay, nay, you will crush my hand!

PEPYS.   I will kiss it away—both of them (*taking the other*) till you give me your lips in self-defence.   (*Drawing her towards him.*)

MRS. KNIGHT.   Oh, you are strong!

PEPYS.   A great lover.   (*He kisses her long on the lips.*)

MRS. KNIGHT (*with a sigh*).   Ah! you have kissed many lips!

PEPYS.   Never! never! . . . I swear it on the head——

MRS. KNIGHT (*laughing softly*).   What! another gift?

PEPYS.   Eh?

MRS. KNIGHT.   A great liar?

PEPYS (*roars with laughter*).   Never lips like yours, I swear it. (*Taking her hands again*).   Song and wit and love together!

MRS. KNIGHT.   A poet, too?   (*Laughing.*)

PEPYS.   I could be anything with you, divine one.   My perfect goddess!   (*About to kiss her again—he rises and goes* c.)   Egad, that reminds me I have a gift——

MRS. KNIGHT.   Yet another gift!

PEPYS.   For you   (*He takes a small packet from his pocket.*) Perfection's final touch to woman's beauty   (*He unrolls a pair of green silk stockings.*)

MRS. KNIGHT (*laughing*).   Green stockings . . . I never wear 'em.

PEPYS.   Faith, they are all the mode and mighty becoming to the leg, I swear.   'Twas but t'other day the Duke of York said, " There is no salvation for a leg save in green stockings."   (*Holding them up.*)

MRS. KNIGHT.   Then I'll wear 'em for your sake.   (*Taking them.*)

PEPYS.   Now?

MRS. KNIGHT. No, no——

PEPYS. Faith, now ; I must see you wear 'em.

MRS. KNIGHT. You are bold !

PEPYS. To desperation.

MRS. KNIGHT. Then turn your back.

PEPYS. But I cannot see you wear 'em if I turn my back.

MRS. KNIGHT. You will never see me wear 'em if you don't.

PEPYS (*turning his back*). Be quick, then, or I shall die of longing.

MRS. KNIGHT (*stripping off a pink stocking*). You have the green sickness ; 'tis not dangerous.

PEPYS (*catching sight of the mirror*). Be not too sure of that ! (*He moves up stage. She pulls on a green stocking. He kisses his hand to the mirror.*)

MRS. KNIGHT. Anticipation is the—Oh, cheat ! (*Catching sight of him in the mirror.*)

PEPYS. In love and war——

MRS. KNIGHT. Go stand like a bad boy with your face to the wall.

(PEPYS *does so* R., *below dressing table.*)

So—that is better !

PEPYS. Oh, for a swivel eye !

MRS. KNIGHT. I feel as if your periwig were as full of eyes as a peacock's tail. (*As she garters the green stocking.*) There—now you may turn.

PEPYS (*turning and gazing rapturously*). Divinity ! (*He comes quickly towards her.*)

MRS. KNIGHT. Down on your knees, then ! (*He kneels a little away from her.*) How do you feel now ?

PEPYS. Like Adam before the green tree of the knowledge of good and evil.

MRS. KNIGHT (*bending forward*). Beware ! I am Eve and the serpent in one.

PEPYS (*holding out his arms*). Paradise ! . . .

(JULIA *bursts in* R., *slamming the door.*)

Hell and damnation ! (*Springing to his feet.*)

JULIA (*breathless*). Madam, the King and Mr. Prodgers coming up the stairs two at a time !

MRS. KNIGHT (*springing up*). Crimine ! I'm undone !

PEPYS (*wildly*). Let me out, let me out ! (*Dashing to door* L.) Let me out !

MRS. KNIGHT. Not there ! It's my bedroom ! Quick, in here ! (*Flinging open the chest.*)

(PEPYS *hurries into it.* JULIA *throws his hat and stick and* MRS. KNIGHT *throws the stockings on top of him.*)

And don't breathe !

PEPYS.   Faith, I shan't be able to.

(*She shuts the lid and sits on the chest arranging her curls as the door flies open and* CHARLES *enters, followed by* PRODGERS.)

CHARLES (*blowing her a kiss*). My Lesbia ! I thought I'd make my visit a surprise.

MRS. KNIGHT (*with a breathless curtsy*). O Sire, you have !

CHARLES (*taking* PRODGERS *familiarly by the ear*). Prodgers shall sit out there and read his prayers.

(PRODGERS *relieves him of his hat and stick.*)

(JULIA *passes out, dropping a curtsy.*)

And mind, Prodgers, see you fast as well as pray . . . don't let me catch you kissing Julia when I come out.

(PRODGERS *retires, closing the door.*)

(CHARLES *goes to* MRS. KNIGHT.)

And so, my dear, you are surprised to see me ?

MRS. KNIGHT.   I was almost surprised, Your Majesty.

CHARLES.   Majesty ! s'life, we are formal !

MRS. KNIGHT.   I have been nearly two years abroad, I have been three weeks home—I thought Your Majesty had forgotten me.

CHARLES.   I had almost forgotten how lovely you are . . . you look as if you had stepped from a canvas of Veronese.

MRS. KNIGHT.   Your Majesty's gallery of beauties is so full, it was easy to forget the Veronese.

CHARLES.   I have forgot 'em all to-day . . . except the frames, egad, which are so expensive I shall have to summon my damned faithful Commons to pay for 'em. (*Crossing to her.*) Come, we are not cross, eh ? (*He raises her chin with his finger. She laughs, then rising, puts her arms round his neck and kisses him.*) I am forgiven, eh ?

MRS. KNIGHT.   I've been hating you for twenty days, Charles, and I'm so tired of it that, faith, I'll love you now for a change. (*Kiss.*)

CHARLES (*stroking her cheek*). Looking like a saint and being a devil within . . . don't I know you ?

MRS. KNIGHT (*laughing*). Oh, no ! You don't know me. (*Crossing* L.) I got a new halo and laid the devil in Italy.

CHARLES.   We shall see about that, i' faith. (*Laughing.*)

MRS. KNIGHT.   I lived in churches and sang at Mass for more Cardinals than I could count.

CHARLES.   I am glad of that. You shall attend the Queen's chapel ; we will arrange it. You always had the serene air, Lesbia,

that is why I loved you, I think. (*Crossing to couch and sitting.*)
I get tired of their racketing at times, and their greed and their
bawdry. Faith, 'tis good to think I can drop in here at any moment,
and find peace and order and beauty. (*Looking round the room,
observing his portrait* R.)

(MRS. KNIGHT *glances at chest.*)

Plague! d'ye still keep that dreadful thing of me!

MRS. KNIGHT. My priceless picture! 'Tis by Hales!

CHARLES. He should hang beside it . . . I look like Paul after
a gaudy night with the Corinthians. (*Turning to her.*) And so
Italy pleased you?

MRS. KNIGHT. Divinely! (*Sitting on chest.*)

CHARLES. We wrote our Ambassadors at Rome and Venice to
have a care of you.

MRS. KNIGHT. I had everything I desired.

CHARLES. And did you go on the lagoons in those ridiculous
little black coffins?

MRS. KNIGHT. Yes, yes.

CHARLES. And sing in the moonlight?

MRS. KNIGHT. Yes.

CHARLES. And ogle the gallants on the Piazza? (*She nods.*)
And eat ratafias? And watch the fireworks? (*She nods.*) Ha!
ha! ha! Odsbud, it makes me long to be young again.

MRS. KNIGHT (*laughing*). Fie! you are as young as ever.

CHARLES. Ay, and as old. And what of Rome; did you see
the Pope?

MRS. KNIGHT. I sang in the Sistine. 'Twas against the rules,
but in Rome they dote on the exception. I had audience next day,
and kissed his ring, and he told me a story . . . something about
angels . . . but he would speak English, so I couldn't understand
him.

(CHARLES *rises, and laughing, goes towards the harpsichord.*)

CHARLES. And how of your singing . . . is it better? . . . As
I remember that is not possible. (*Picking up "Beauty Retire."*)

MRS. KNIGHT. I worked every day . . . but you shall judge for
yourself.

CHARLES (*who has picked up the sheet of music from the harpsichord,
reading*). "'Beauty Retire,' etcetra, being set to music by Samuel
Pepys." Samuel Pepys! Sure this cannot be the dull fellow of the
Admiralty who plagues me with letters as long as the day o' judg-
ment.

MRS. KNIGHT. 'Tis Mr. Pepys of the Navy Office, that is all I
know.

CHARLES. Egad, then 'tis the same! (*He laughs heartily, coming
down* C.) This is the eighth wonder of the world! Samuel Pepys

. . . a writer of songs ! The dullest dog you could meet in a day, ha ! ha ! ha ! But you know him to be sure ?

MRS. KNIGHT. I have met him but once.

CHARLES. And once too often, I'll wager. I have seen him once and again. Oh, a very worthy man, most diligent in service and honest. James thinks highly of him in naval matters, but odslife, what a dullard, a Puritan in a periwig (*turns up to harpsichord*), mum as a sexton at a funeral. (*Throws down the paper.*) And so he writes songs ! Ha ! ha ! ha ! (*Coming down to couch again.*) Egad, I'll twit him with it when I see him next. Come sing to me, sweetheart. (*Lies on couch.*)

MRS. KNIGHT (*at the harpsichord*). What would you have ? (*With a smile.*) " Beauty Retire " ? (*As he stretches himself on the day bed* R.)

CHARLES. Heaven forbid ! 'Twould set me thinking of his memorandum of last week. One sentence two hundred and seventy words ! Faith, I had to call for chocolate after the twenty-third comma, and broke into a sweat before I reached the full stop. (*Laughing.*) No, something to make me forget him.

(MRS. KNIGHT *sings "Early one morning." Early in the song* CHARLES *raises himself on his elbow, watching her.*)

CHARLES. Egad, the Pope was in the right about the angel. (*Taking his feet from couch.*) You must sing at Whitehall . . . to-morrow . . . I will send Grabu to arrange it. (*He sits staring in front of him. Then suddenly :*) What is that gaudy gilded coffin for ? (*He comes forward, bending down to examine it.*)

MRS. KNIGHT (*rising quickly*). That ? Oh, 'tis a marriage chest . . . 'twas painted for me in Parma—by Zacchiotto. (*She slips between him and the chest, sitting on it, facing him.*)

CHARLES. A marriage chest—hah ! Where you will hide your husbands when I come to see you, eh ?

MRS. KNIGHT. I shall have no husband while you come to see me.

CHARLES (*sitting beside her*). Sweet sweetheart, you are the best of 'em all . . . for I believe you love me, and are true to me when I am not by. As for the rest, I know I wear a forest of antlers by them. But what o' that, they are not planted deep, so I shake my head care-free when I come to you. (*He kisses her, then whispers.*) Shall I stay with you to-night ?

PRODGERS (*without*). No, no, indeed, madam, no.

(*A shrill angry woman's voice is heard in the ante-room.*)

MRS. PEPYS (*without*). I know he is . . . I say I must !

PRODGERS (*without*). Not in there, madam !—on your life !

(CHARLES *rises, moving up* R.C. *The door bursts open, and* MRS. PEPYS *forces herself in with* PRODGERS *trying to drag her back by*

her cloak ; quickly she unfastens the hook at her neck. PRODGERS
*falls, sitting with the cloak in his hands. She slams the door, locks
it, and leans panting against it.* CHARLES, *unseen by her, slips
quietly behind the window curtains* R.C. MRS. KNIGHT *rises.*
PRODGERS *hammers on the door outside.)*

(*Without.*) Come out, madam, come out, come out ! . . . open the
door ! . . . you must come out ! (*More knocking.*)

MRS. KNIGHT. How dare you thrust yourself into my house,
madam ? Who are you, and what do you want ?

MRS. PEPYS. I am Mistress Pepys, and I want my husband.

PRODGERS. Madam, you *must* come out. (*Knocking.*)

MRS. KNIGHT. Leave my house ! This is insolence . . . your
husband is not here.

MRS. PEPYS (*taking the key from the lock*). By your leave, I will
find that out for myself. (*She puts the key in the bosom of her
dress.*)

PRODGERS. Woman, if you do not come out, I must send for
the watch. (*Knocking.*)

MRS. PEPYS (R.C.). Now then, enough of this ! I want my
husband—where is he ?

MRS. KNIGHT. How should I know, insolence ! (*Sitting on chest.*)
I've never seen you before, how do I know you have a husband ?

MRS. PEPYS. Very pert indeed, madam. Have *you* ?

MRS. KNIGHT. No, but if I had, I'd have the wit to keep him
at home.

MRS. PEPYS. Wit indeed ! If you've had the impudence to take
mine (*stepping towards* MRS. KNIGHT), I'll scratch your eyes out.

MRS. KNIGHT (*laughing and rising*). A fish-wife, i' faith !

MRS. PEPYS. You are Mistress Knight, the singing woman, are
you not ?

MRS. KNIGHT. I am, and what then ?

MRS. PEPYS (*shows her the paper which she takes from her dress*).
And that is the address of your lodging ? (*Giving paper to* MRS
KNIGHT.)

MRS. KNIGHT. Yes.

MRS. PEPYS. And writ in your own hand ?

MRS. KNIGHT. It seems so.

MRS. PEPYS. Seems, i' faith !

(MRS. PEPYS *snatches paper from* MRS. KNIGHT.)

Well, it *seems* I found this on my husband's table.

MRS. KNIGHT. And if you did . . . I did not put it there.

MRS. PEPYS. No, but you gave it him.

MRS. KNIGHT. I did not.

MRS. PEPYS (*going* R.). I know he consorts with singing people
and music-makers and players and all such flimsy riffraff.

Mrs. Knight. Pray you, keep a civil tongue in your head. Why,
I may have given it to a dozen hands—to—to friends at the court
or——

Mrs. Pepys. Lord, how fine !

Mrs. Knight. Or players at the King's house or the Duke's
. . . to Moone or Cartwright, Hart, Lacy, Kynaston—to Mistress
Marshall, to Mistress Corey, to Mistress Knepp——

Mrs. Pepys (*suddenly crestfallen*). Knepp ! Oh ! . . . you know
her ?

Mrs. Knight. Faith, very well. Ay, now I mind me . . . it
was Tuesday last . . . ay, so it was . . . she asked me where I
lodged . . . I gave her such a slip of paper, and wrote upon it.

Mrs. Pepys (*after a look in her eyes*). I don't believe you. He
did not put on his coloured coat and flowered tabby vest to go to
the Navy Office.

Mrs. Knight. Coloured tabby cats ! (*Crosses above chest to door*
L.) You silly jealous fool ! Because you cannot keep your husband
at home, must he be here ?   I'm not your husband's keeper !

Mrs. Pepys. No, but I doubt he's yours !

Mrs. Knight. This is past all bearing. Take yourself off, madam,
he is not here as you can see.

Mrs. Pepys. Yes, when I've seen in there ! (*She darts towards*
door L.)

Mrs. Knight (*intercepting her*). That is my bedroom, madam.

Mrs. Pepys. And just where I'd expect to find him.

Mrs. Knight. A plague on all women who cannot keep their
husbands to themselves ! (*Throwing open the door.*) There !
Search, madam, search my room since you insist, and much good
may it do you.

(Mrs. Pepys *goes into the room.* Mrs. Knight *stands outside*
looking in.)

Look well in there . . . (*basket is overturned*) aye, and in that dark
corner too (*dragging a chair*) . . . search under the bed, madam, if
you're convinced he isn't in it (*boxes moved*) . . . and in my ward-
robe, he may be hiding behind my petticoats (*chair overturned*) . . .
and don't forget the ceiling . . . look up there . . . among the
flies.

Charles (*in a whisper, sticking his head out*). Lock her in, lock
her in, and egad we'll have some sport !

(Mrs. Knight *rushes towards him waving him back. He disappears.*
As she turns to come down the lid of the chest rises, and Pepys' *head*
appears panting for breath. She sits on the lid as Mrs. Pepys *comes*
crestfallen from the room.)

Mrs. Knight. Well, now, I hope you're satisfied.

Mrs. Pepys. I hope I am. But just let him wait till he comes home.

(Mrs. Knight *rises, laughing.*)

Mrs. Knight. Till he comes home! Poor man, I pity him. (*Going to door* R.)

Mrs. Pepys. He can do without your pity, madam.

Mrs. Knight (*turning*). No doubt, no doubt! And now, Mistress Pepys, perhaps *you* will go home and wait for *him*. I think you have the key.

(Mrs. Pepys *crosses* R., *vainly trying to extract the key from her corsage.*)

Mrs. Pepys (*down by foot of couch*). I think the key has slipped.

Mrs. Knight (*on her* R.). Evil communications . . . and now it hides for shame.

Mrs. Pepys (*with venom*). Do not you preach at *me* . . . I knew you were a hussy by your face. (*She turns her back on* Mrs. Knight and *struggles for the key.*)

Mrs. Knight (*laughing*). Oh, manners! Shall I send for a locksmith, or would you have it fished out with a hook and line?

(*Suddenly the curtains on the window are shaken by a movement.* Mrs. Pepys *sees it and with a cry rushes at them, too quick for* Mrs. Knight, *who tries to grab her.*)

Mrs. Pepys (*throwing back the curtains*). He's here! Come out, you dog!

(Charles *stands vastly amused.* Mrs. Pepys *stares open-mouthed, then staggers back, dropping a terrified curtsy.*)

Your Majesty (*backing down to below chest*)—Oh Lord!

Charles (*coming forward to* C.). So this is Mistress Pepys—egad, they have damned good taste in the Navy . . . Pepys is a connoisseur.

Mrs. Pepys (*tremblingly*). Your Majesty—I—I—forgive me . . . I am a fool. (*Giving a deep curtsy.*)

Charles (*coming in front of chest and helping her to rise*). A vastly pretty one, I'll swear. But if *you* suspect your husband, faith you are a fool. *You* jealous! Fie, look in your glass, Mistress Pepys. I warrant he has more cause a hundredfold to be jealous of you.

Mrs. Pepys. I never gave him none.

Charles. And I'll vow he gives you less. What! suspect my worthy Pepys? Faith, I'd sooner suspect the Archbishop of Canterbury myself . . . or York or—(*to* Mrs. Knight *with a grin*)—he's got a roguish eye let me tell you that same York! But honest Pepys! A good man if ever I saw one, and a sober, and a pious—says his prayers I doubt not——

Mrs. Pepys. Yes, yes.

CHARLES. I knew it. The most diligent, the dull—most devoted, the most proper man I know. (*Laughing.*) Egad, I can't imagine Pepys ever looking at a woman.

(MRS. KNIGHT *turns to fireplace.*)

MRS. PEPYS. You don't know him, Your Majesty.

CHARLES (*laughing*). Oho, don't I! (*Looking at her.*) And yet he had the wit to pick a mighty pretty wife! (*To* MRS. KNIGHT.) Or is that the mark of a fool in these days? Tell me, Mistress Pepys, what caused you to suspect that he was here?

MRS. PEPYS. This paper . . . which is written in her hand. (*Giving paper to* CHARLES.)

CHARLES. Do you admit the writing? (*To* MRS. KNIGHT.)

MRS. KNIGHT (*moving towards couch, calmly*). Why, yes . . . but I have written dozens like it.

MRS. PEPYS. I found it on the table, in our house.

CHARLES. So I heard—but does that prove that it was given to Pepys?

MRS. PEPYS. Who was it given to then?

CHARLES. Mistress Knight has told you—to Mistress Knepp.

(MRS. KNIGHT *turns again to fireplace.*)

MRS. PEPYS. Humph!

CHARLES. Had Mistress Knepp been at your house?

MRS. PEPYS (*sullenly*). Yes. (*Bursting out.*) Though he'd sworn he'd never see her again!

CHARLES. When was she last there?

MRS. PEPYS (*reluctantly*). To-day, Your Majesty. When I came home . . . I found her there——

CHARLES. Before you found the paper? (*Giving it again to* MRS. PEPYS.)

MRS. PEPYS. Yes, Your Majesty.

CHARLES. *Probatum est*! Odsbud! Madam, do you not see how your suspicion has wronged Mistress Knight—and wrongs your husband, too? Mistress Pepys, I fear you are a jealous woman.

MRS. PEPYS. I have cause.

CHARLES. That may be in the spleen! What! Suspect your husband because he goes out without you!

MRS. PEPYS. He told me he was going to the Navy Office——

CHARLES. And most like he was.

MRS. PEPYS. But he isn't there . . . I couldn't get in——

CHARLES. Then how d'ye know he isn't there?

MRS. PEPYS. I knocked and knocked——

CHARLES. He did not hear. The Navy Office! depend on't he is there. Faith, from the infernal length of his letters, he must be there, ploughing seas of ink, from cockcrow till midnight. And is this all?

MRS. PEPYS. Please, Your Majesty . . . before he went out he put on his best clothes——

CHARLES. Oh, did he so?

MRS. PEPYS. And . . . and he took his flageolet.

CHARLES. Took his flageolet?

MRS. PEPYS. Yes, Your Majesty.

CHARLES. What the devil did he do that for?

MRS. PEPYS. He plays, Your Majesty . . . he's mightily fond of music.

CHARLES. I see. Humph! Mistress Pepys, we find you have no grounds for your suspicions. If your husband took his flageolet he may be guilty of music, but of nothing worse. Go home, and take this word in your ear—'tis our eleventh commandment—" Wife, suspect not thy husband "! Would all the jealous wives of England might hear me, so the peace of our realm, which is our chief concern (*turning up to head of couch*), might be preserved.

(MRS. KNIGHT *goes to door.*)

MRS. PEPYS (*curtsying*). But, Your Majesty, . . . if one has cause to suspect?

CHARLES (*turning to her*). Not unless you have proof, and then 'tis no longer suspicion. Good night.

(MRS. KNIGHT *has already gone to the door.* MRS. PEPYS *drops a curtsy and follows.*)

MRS. KNIGHT. And now, madam, without proof may I suspect that you still have the key?

(MRS. PEPYS *dives her hand into her bodice and begins again her struggle to recapture it.* CHARLES *comes down, smiling.*)

CHARLES. May *we* exercise a royal prerogative?

MRS. KNIGHT. Your Majesty, the property is on territory where the King's writ does not run.

CHARLES. Odso! (*Laughing.*) Then egad we will turn our back till Mistress Pepys can digest the key.

(*He goes up behind the harpsichord while* MRS. KNIGHT *and* MRS. PEPYS *between them work the key out of her bodice. Suddenly he sees the flageolet on the harpsichord—picks it up, exclaiming under his breath :*)

The devil he is!

(*He turns with it in his hand, about to speak, then changing his mind, turns, looks behind the curtains of the window L., glances round the room, and as his eye falls on the chest, comes down smiling, and while* MRS. KNIGHT *is putting the key in the door he lifts the lid of the chest a little way and peeps in. Then slipping the flageolet into his pocket, he drops on the R. end of the chest, shaking with laughter.*)

At this point Mrs. Knight *has turned the lock.   Both turn towards him at the sound of the laugh.)*

Mistress Pepys . . . a moment . . . come hither, a thought—a merry thought has struck me.

(Mrs. Pepys *comes over nervously to his* r.)

Nay, nay, sit here beside me. *(Tapping the chest.   She sits on his* l. *timidly.*   Mrs. Knight *stands watching anxiously.)*   Touching these home affairs 'twixt you and Pepys . . . I have seen a doubt . . . a grave doubt . . . I may disclose it presently.   I have been less than just to you.   We will reopen the case.   Now, while suspicion in a wife is damnable, and the cause of great uneasiness at home, it may be that she has so many reasons for suspicion as to put her in the right.

Mrs. Pepys.   Faith, I've enough of them and to spare.

Charles.   Suspicious circumstance in mass, amounts to proof in law.

Mrs. Pepys.   I know nothing of law, but if Your Majesty had lived with him these five years past and seen his nose lift like a pointer's at every petticoat in the wind, you wouldn't want the law to tell you what he'd be at.   And then——   *(She stops, confused at her familiarity.)*

Charles.   Go on.

Mrs. Pepys.   And then the cunning of him.   I'd need to be all eyes to catch him, and when I do catch him he wriggles out of it. You ought to have just seen the women, Your Majesty—women is too good for them, the——   *(She stops again.)*

Charles.   Go on, go on—this interests us.

Mrs. Pepys.   There was Mrs. Daniels, one of the first, a bold-eyed brassy wench whose husband kept to sea——

Charles *(with a sigh)*.   The Navy has much to answer for.

Mrs. Pepys.   I saw him cuddle her in the garden behind the washing on the line.   Would you believe it ?

Charles.   Tsch ! tsch ! tsch !   *(Slapping the chest.)*   Bad rogue ! *(To* Mrs. Knight.)   We could scarce believe this, eh ?   Could we, Lesbia ?

(Mrs. Knight *turns away angrily and sits at the dressing-table.)*

Mrs. Pepys.   And Betty Turner, forward puss ! . . . and Mistress Pierce, the painted hussy ! . . . ogling and whispering in their ears and squeezing their hands.

Charles *(slapping the chest)*.   Rascal !   Rascal ! . . .   Hear you that, Lesbia ?   The sober Pepys !   *(Laughing.)*

Mrs. Pepys.   And Mistress Knepp——

Charles.   Babs Knepp !   Is't possible !   *(Trying to restrain his laughter.)*

Mrs. Pepys *(nodding)*.   He kissed the back of her neck, and swore he was but smelling of a new perfume she had upon her hair.

CHARLES. Monstrous! monstrous! Poaching in the Playhouse, egad! The villain!

MRS. PEPYS. And our maids, Jane . . . and Deb Willett—I know he went lengths with her—and all our maids. . . . Why, this very day I caught him kissing Lettice on the mouth, and she not two weeks in the house.

CHARLES (*with great slap on the chest*). The old rascally goat! (*He bursts out laughing.*) Would you have thought it, Lesbia? Not two weeks in the house! Grave Pepys!—worthy Pepys!—pious Pepys! A writer of songs, too! (*Laughs, then checks himself.*) Fie, fie, 'tis a shame! False to such a sweet pretty adorable face! The man's a monster! Egad, you've proved the crime, my dear—ay, to the hilt. I'll pass sentence on him myself, and you shall be his executioner.

MRS. PEPYS (*rising*). Oh, I would not have him hanged——

CHARLES (*laughing*). Nay, horned, not hanged (*he draws her on to the chest again*)—hanging's too good for him. What! a man who neglects the beauty by his side! Pay him out, my dear, let him see that other men know the worth he ignores. (*Taking her hand.*) 'Tis bare justice! 'Tis the law of love, my dear . . . an eye for an eye, a tooth for a tooth . . . a kiss for a kiss. 'Tis equity!

MRS. PEPYS. Faith, there have been some who would have, an' they could.

CHARLES (*stroking her hand*). I'll be bound there have. This slender, branching arm, and blossoming white fingers. The man's a fool to go picking flowers in other fields.

(MRS. PEPYS *rises.*)

Look, Lesbia, is it not a white dainty hand?

MRS. KNIGHT (*struggling between jealousy and rage*). If Your Majesty says so, alabaster!

MRS. PEPYS (*half pleased but afraid*). Your Majesty is laughing at me.

CHARLES. Faith, I laugh in delight of you. (*He draws her on to chest again. Coming closer to her.*) Who would not long for those pretty pouting lips . . . and a shape might tempt an anchorite——

MRS. PEPYS (*laughing*). Oh, Your Majesty!

CHARLES. Faith and troth 'tis so! Has she not a jewel of a mouth, Lesbia? Coral set with pearls!

(MRS. KNIGHT *in fury turns her back on them.*)

MRS. PEPYS (*laughing*). Nay! nay!

CHARLES. And when you laugh, the dimples, egad! (*Touching them with his fingers.*) Like roguish cupids playing hide-and-seek.

MRS. PEPYS (*laughing*). I . . . can't . . . help laughing . . . you tickle my face so ! (*She laughs again and he with her.*)

CHARLES (*dropping his voice*). And your eyes . . . when I look in your eyes . . . lakes of blue fire, i' faith, with little devils sitting in the corners of 'em. Aha ! you laugh at that, eh ? Enchanting rogue ! I'll wager you're full of little devils, eh ?

MRS. PEPYS (*laughing*). No . . . no . . . indeed I'm not.

CHARLES (*slipping an arm round her waist*). Yes, yes, I've seen some of 'em in your eyes. Odsbud ! (*Giving a kick with his heel on the chest.*) If Pepys could but hear how better men desire those lips, he might pipe another tune. And I am one of 'em, egad . . . and we'll set our royal seal on a bargain between us. (*He kisses her loudly on the lips.*)

(MRS. KNIGHT, *who has been watching in the mirror, springs to her feet and goes up to the window* R. MRS. PEPYS, *sobered, covers her face with her hands.* CHARLES *rises.*)

Mistress Pepys—(*she looks up*)—you have made your King your slave. We promise you anything you may ask—anything, on our royal faith, and if Pepys be faithless send to us and we'll redeem the pledge. (*He bows to her. She rises, curtsying. He crosses to the door, calling.*) Prodgers ! Prodgers !

PRODGERS (*throwing open the door*). Your Majesty !

CHARLES. Conduct Mistress Pepys to a coach. Show her your best consideration, Prodgers. (*Turning to* MRS. PEPYS, *who has followed, he leads her to door.*) Mistress Pepys, we shall have a special care of you. If ever you should desire revenge, a word to me and it is yours.

MRS. PEPYS (*curtsying*). Your Majesty !

CHARLES (*raising her*). And do not forget the seal is on our bond. (*He kisses her hand.*)

MRS. PEPYS. I shall not forget, Your Majesty.

CHARLES. Fare you well.

(MRS. PEPYS *backs out.* PRODGERS *closes the door.*)

(*Turns to* MRS. KNIGHT.) And now, my Lesbia——

MRS. KNIGHT (*in a fury*). Do not speak to me ! To make love to her . . . before my very face . . . (*Coming down* L.)

CHARLES. And behind your beautiful back, egad——

MRS. KNIGHT. It's outrageous !

CHARLES. Hoity-toity !

MRS. KNIGHT. The minx ! . . . the insult ! . . . I'd have thrown her out if——

CHARLES. Fie ! Separate husband and wife ? (*Pointing.*) Open that chest !

MRS. KNIGHT (*facing him*). Do you dare——

CHARLES (*thundering*). Woman ! Open that chest !

(*She looks him in the eyes a moment, then draws herself up, turns, and lifts up the lid of the chest. There is no movement in the chest.*)

(*With a laugh.*) Where you hide your husbands, eh ? (*She lets the lid drop on floor and goes up above harpsichord. Still no movement in the chest.*) Peste ! is the fellow dead ? (*Loudly.*) Samuel, come forth !

(*It is a very crestfallen* PEPYS *whose head emerges slowly above the edge of the chest, periwig somewhat awry, half suffocated, and pale with anger and jealousy. He stares half frightened, half furious, at the* KING.)

So this is what you do while I'm reading your damned long letters about the Navy !

PEPYS (*getting up, panting*). If Your Majesty will wait till I recover my wind I will answer you shortly. (*Stepping out of the chest.*)

CHARLES. Wind, faith, you'll need a *hurricane*, you have so much to answer. (*He bursts out laughing.*) Put . . . your periwig . . . straight, or I shall die o' laughing.

(PEPYS, *still panting, pulls his wig straight.*)

That's better ! So, Master Pepys, we thought you a Puritan, but it would seem you are a gallant, a raffish coxcomb, a gay gadder, a Don Juan, a Grand Turk, a devil with the women, in short—what do you mean, sir, by poaching on my preserves ?

PEPYS (*still panting*). Your Majesty, I protest . . . I came here out of love . . . of music . . . which I esteem above anything in the world . . . to hear this lady sing. (*He turns towards* MRS. KNIGHT, *and reveals a green stocking adhering to the back of his coat.*)

CHARLES (*moving up to* PEPYS, *with a laugh*). Sing, say you ! Odsbud, then 'tis a pity you can't see behind you. (*Picking the stocking off and dangling it in front of him.*) So this is the music you love so . . . a pretty duet with one part missing !

PEPYS. I can explain, Your Majesty . . . (*Stepping back* L. *to chest.*)

CHARLES. Faith, you can explain yourself out of any bed in England, we are told. (*Going* R.)

PEPYS. I was but following the precept of Your Majesty's brother : " There is no salvation for a leg save in green stockings——"

CHARLES (*laughing*). Another hypocrite, egad !

PEPYS. And venturing to make a trifling gift to Mistress Knight, she put one on to please me, while I turned my back. (*Turning to* L.)

CHARLES. And pleased yourself by peeping round the corner.

PEPYS (*turning to* CHARLES). Fie ! Your Majesty, the suggestion is unworthy.

CHARLES. You old sinner ! What were you doing in that chest ?

PEPYS (*losing his temper*). Trying to breathe, and getting cramp :n every inch of my body !

CHARLES (*laughing*). Faith, had I known that, you'd have stayed there all night. (*Sternly.*) Come, no equivocation, answer my question on your peril.

PEPYS (*sullenly*). I have told Your Majesty the truth already.

CHARLES. Humph !

PEPYS. I came to hear Mistress Knight sing . . . there is no music lover—and I am not the least—who would not have leapt at the chance.

CHARLES. But you leapt in the chest.

PEPYS. My one false step, for which I humbly pray Mistress Knight's forgiveness. (*Bowing to her.*)

CHARLES. Mistress Knight's forgiveness, sir ?

PEPYS. Your Majesty's sudden coming was to blame.

CHARLES. Eh ?

PEPYS. I know not whether I felt you would be shocked to find the brave, worthy, diligent, *dull* Pepys at music in a lady's chamber . . . or that you would be displeased to find her not alone, or what I felt, but without a pause for thought, I slipped into the chest.

CHARLES. Force of habit, egad ! And the lady helped you in, I'll wager.

PEPYS. I was too quick for her, Your Majesty. I was in before she knew. In Your Majesty's presence it would have been unseemly to pull me out.

CHARLES (*turning to* MRS. KNIGHT). And you, madam—do you endorse these lies ?

MRS. KNIGHT. If Your Majesty is incapable of believing truth, I prefer to be silent.

CHARLES. So ! You cannot lie ! Yet you lied like a lawyer to Mistress Pepys.

MRS. KNIGHT. I used a woman's only weapon to rid Your Majesty of an unwelcome intruder.

CHARLES (*moving to* R.). Egad ! Between the two of you you'll persuade me presently I am not here.

PEPYS. Your Majesty is here, and it would be a blessed chance if I could persuade you to your good——

CHARLES. To my good ?

PEPYS. Ay, Your Majesty, and the good of your realm. You have heard much to-night of my faults, my foibles, the sins we men who have a devil in us strive to hide from our wives ; Your Majesty has called me gadder, Grand Turk, a devil among the women— I'll not deny it. But, besides, I serve Your Majesty with all my might ay, from cockcrow till midnight four days out of five. Yet what avails this labour and that of many others ? . . . but little while the Navy—

(CHARLES *turns to him.*)

—is starved. We may want ships and stores and guns, but we know that my Lady Castlemaine—

(CHARLES *crosses* R. *to fireplace.*)

—needs clothes and pearls and plate. Our seamen may want their pay—this very morning a crowd of them, poor brave men, clamoured before the office—but we know that the women, the false friends, the rogues who bleed Your Majesty, must have theirs first——

CHARLES (*turning and cutting him short*). Zoons, sir! You do forget yourself!

PEPYS. I have but one head to lose, and in Your Majesty's service I will gladly lay it down.

(CHARLES *comes* L. *to foot of couch.*)

Your Majesty's realm is set upon the sea, sustained by the ships of your fleet, and if you starve them we must sink.

CHARLES (*crossing* L. *to chest and throwing in the stockings*). Mr. Pepys, we are not in council—you have leave to go.

PEPYS. I am Your Majesty's most humble, devoted and obedient servant. (*Bowing.*) I beg you believe it.

(CHARLES *crosses away to table* L.)

(*Picking his hat and stick out of the chest and going to* MRS. KNIGHT.)

Mistress Knight (*she moves down to him*), if this day I did you some slight service, pray let it be remembered to excuse my foolishness to-night. While I live I shall not forget your singing.

MRS. KNIGHT (*giving him her hand to kiss*). I am still your debtor, Mr. Pepys, more than I can say.

(PEPYS *goes towards door* R.)

CHARLES (*turning*). Ay, and forget not what I said to Mistress Pepys, if you heard it all.

PEPYS (*turning to* CHARLES). I heard Your Majesty—I had not room to blush.

CHARLES (*when* PEPYS *is almost at the door* R.). Faith, see you have a care for the future, then—what would you say if Mistress Pepys should one day ask for her revenge?

PEPYS (*bursting out*). I should say . . . (*he masters himself, then smiles and bows*) *Honi soit qui mal y pense*, Your Majesty.

(*He goes out by the door* R.)

CHARLES (*crossing towards the couch* R.C.). Prodgers!

(MRS. KNIGHT *sits at the harpsichord, ignoring him.*)

(PRODGERS *opens the door.*)

My coach!

PRODGERS (*bowing*). Very good, Your Majesty. (*He closes the door.*)

(MRS. KNIGHT *strums a few bars.* CHARLES *goes up to the window R., where he stands in the moonlight, with his back to her, looking out. She turns over pages, strums again, and cautiously peeping round, sees he has his back to her. Turns over more pages and hums to herself. A pause.*)

CHARLES (*dryly*). What was this " slight service " that he did you ?

MRS. KNIGHT (*after a few bars*). Oh . . . he saved my life.

CHARLES. Ha ! . . . (*She strums.*) How, pray ?

MRS. KNIGHT. From a pick-purse who would have murdered me. (*Strum.*) He near beat the ruffian to death—though the fellow escaped. (*Strum.*) Most like the watch have him by now.

CHARLES. So the rascal has courage . . . as well as impudence.

(*She strums and hums a few bars.*)

The damnedest liar in London, egad ! (*Sitting in chair by dressing-table.*)

MRS. KNIGHT. All that he said to Your Majesty was true. (*Strums.*)

CHARLES. Have you the face to say that to me ?

MRS. KNIGHT. I could say it facing you. But Your Majesty's sense of right is so perverse you would not see it.

CHARLES. What d'ye mean ?

MRS. KNIGHT. Your Majesty has listened to lies so long, I fear you have forgotten the sound of truth.

CHARLES. Egad, they all lie to me, and that is true.

(*She looks at him, closes the book, rises and blows out the candle on the harpsichord.*)

MRS. KNIGHT. Good night, Your Majesty. (*Without looking at him.*)

CHARLES (*stiffly*). We have not left yet.

MRS. KNIGHT. As Your Majesty pleases. (*She resumes her seat. A pause. She picks out a tune with one finger.*)

CHARLES. I know they all lie to me . . . and I thought that you did not. (*A pause.*) Well ?

MRS. KNIGHT. Your Majesty has offended me. You have not asked my pardon. I cannot speak.

CHARLES (*rising, amazed*). I ask your pardon ! (*Laughs.*)

(*She rises and goes down L., takes candle at table L. in her R. hand.*)

Come, come, tell me all, and I'll believe you, ay, forgive you too.

MRS. KNIGHT (*taking the candle from table*). I have told Your

Majesty . . . till you do me justice, I do not care to speak with you, to see you—or anything.

(Prodgers *enters* r., *carrying the* King's *hat, cloak, and stick.* Charles *stands irresolute.*)

Good night, Your Majesty ! (*She curtsies, moving up to bedroom* l., *and half closing the door.*)

Prodgers. Your Majesty's coach.

Charles (*testily*). Tell 'em to go to the devil ! (*Turning up to dressing-table.*)

(Mrs. Knight *laughs to herself as she closes the door.*)

Prodgers. Very good, Your Majesty. (*Goes to door* r.)

Charles. Oh, Prodgers !

(Prodgers *turns.*)

Mr. Pepys has forgotten his flageolet. (*He takes it from his pocket and gives it him.*) Take care of it, Prodgers, we will decide later what we will do with it.

(Prodgers *again goes to door.* Charles *takes the remaining candle from the dressing-table.*)

And oh, Prodgers !

(Prodgers *turns at the door.*)

The next wild woman who tries to dart past you, grab her round the neck—don't let her leave her cloak in your hands—Mistress Potiphar was a novice.

Prodgers. Very good, Your Majesty ! (*Goes out, closing the door.*)

Charles (*going* l.). And so—— (*He yawns at* c.)

CURTAIN.

ACT III

SCENE.—*The same as Act I. Room in* PEPYS' *House. Supper is nearly over.* MRS. PEPYS *at the* L. *end of the table, with* PELHAM HUMFREY *on her* R. *A branched candlestick in the* C. *of the table. The* BOY *is pouring out the wine from a silver flagon.* DOLL *carries out the dishes of salmon and lobster to the kitchen* R., *leaving the meat dishes for the* GIRLS *and* BOY, *who eat bits with their fingers while they are not serving the table. The company, save* MRS. PEPYS, *are pretty merry.*

(*As the* CURTAIN *rises,* PELLING, CÆSAR, MRS. KNEPP *and* MRS. PIERCE *are laughing heartily,* HUMFREY *leaning back with the conceited smile of a man who has just told a good story.*)

HUMFREY. Yes, *ma foi !* he said it quick . . . quick. (*Snapping his fingers.*) *Comme ça !* (*Turning to* MRS. PEPYS.) *N'est-ce-pas, c'est amusant ?* Oh, His Majesty has a pretty wit—for an Englishman, *pardie !*

MRS. KNEPP. Take that back, you saucy chatterbox. (*Throwing a bit of bread at him.*)

HUMFREY (*dodging it, laughing*). *Eh bien, oui,* I take it back . . . I take it back . . . he has all the wit there is in England. But you know that, Mistress Pepys, you have heard him ?

MRS. PEPYS (*roused*). Oh ! . . . I . . . no . . . I don't remember. What's o'clock, Pelling ?

PELLING (*pulling out his watch*). Past eleven . . . a little.

MRS. PEPYS. Eleven !

HUMFREY. And Monsieur Pepys still abroad. Oh, la, la ! And we have eaten everything.

MRS. PIERCE (*smiling fatuously*). Oh, fie ! . . . Speak for yourself !

DOLL (*at door* R., *wiping her hands on her apron*). Whisht ! girl, bring me dat veal till I keep it hot for massa.

(SUE *brings her the dish of veal.*)

MRS. PIERCE (*whom wine has made precious*). I always think, Mr. Humfrey, that wit is the cream of wine as it were, do not you ? . . . It rises to the top, so to speak. (*She giggles.*)

HUMFREY. *Mon Dieu !* madame, that is very witty. . . . Where did you *hear* that ?

MRS. KNEPP. In Sedley's play last week. And I wanted to say "it depended on the cow who drank it," but they wouldn't let me.

MRS. PIERCE (*hiccoughs, then*). Ouf! 'Tis very hot! (*Fanning herself with her hands.*)

HUMFREY (*tenderly*). *Chère Madame Pepys,* you are *triste.* What is the matter? (*Stroking her hand.*)

MRS. PEPYS. Nothing—I am tired, I think. Mr. Cæsar, the wine stays with you!

MRS. PIERCE (*giggling as* CÆSAR *fills he glass—rising*). Oh, fie! . . . no . . . no . . . no . . . no. The least little drop! (*Sits.*)

MRS. KNEPP. Go on, Cæsar! She likes it in a bucket.

MRS. PIERCE. Oh, you toad! (*To* MRS. PEPYS.) I'll vow, poor soul, you're anxious about Mr. Pepys.

MRS. PEPYS (*sharply*). Not in the least, ma'am.

PELLING. Did the King *wait* to hear you sing, Mr. Humfrey?

HUMFREY. *Vraiment,* no . . . he was gone an hour before I came. . . . I am very cross with him.

MRS. KNEPP. Oh, tut! tut!

HUMFREY (*to* MRS. PEPYS). And I shall tell him so when I see him; *ma foi,* yes. I talk to him like that, you know, I treat him as a man.

MRS. KNEPP. And what does he treat you as . . . a woman? (*Laughing.*)

(BOY *exits, taking dish from chest* R.)

HUMFREY. *Ventre St. Gris!* (*Laughing.*) What a rogue you are, madam! *Vous me faites rire toujours!*

MRS. PEPYS. Tell me, Mistress Knepp, are you acquainted with a Mistress Knight, the singing woman?

MRS. KNEPP. I have spoke to her once or twice.

MRS. PEPYS. Did she ever give you a paper with the address of her lodging?

MRS. KNEPP. Me? Oh, la, no!

(PELLING *pokes her violently in the back.*)

Oh, wait now . . . I remember she did . . . the last time I saw her, and asked me to visit her.

MRS. PEPYS. Where does she lodge?

(HUMFREY *fills* MRS. PIERCE'S *glass.*)

MRS. KNEPP. I have forgot . . . near the City somewhere. . . . I haven't been. (*To* HUMFREY, *who is filling* MRS. PIERCE'S *glass.*) Here! me too! (*Holding out her glass.*)

HUMFREY. You should drink champagne, Madame Pierce. *Délicieuse!* and such tickling in the mouth.

MRS. PIERCE. Tickling (*rising*) . . . Lord, no, I dare not . . . I tickle so easily. If you but bring your hand near me I go off at once (*sitting*) . . . he ! he ! he ! he !

MRS. KNEPP (*as she drains her glass*). Come ! Another song ! Come . . . " When I was a bachelor."

(*All sing except* MRS. PEPYS. *Before the song has gone far,* PEPYS' *voice is heard off.*)

PEPYS (*off*). Boy, boy, Jacke . . . here ! take my things.

(MRS. PEPYS *rises.*)

(SUE *rushes to the kitchen door calling,* " Jacke ! Jacke ! ")

MRS. KNEPP. Here he comes !
HUMFREY. *Ce guillard,* Pepys, *enfin !*
MRS. PIERCE. The poor dear man !

(*Together.*)

(PEPYS *enters laden with large bundles of papers besides his satchel.*)

PEPYS. At last, at last . . . Such a pother of business. I thought I'd never get home ! How do ye all ?

(*He is received with cries of delight from those at the table.*)

MRS. PIERCE. Oh, dear man, we thought you were never coming.
HUMFREY. Ah, Mr. Pepys at last !
MRS. KNEPP. Sweet creature !
PELLING. So you *have* come !

(*And out of the end of the hubbub the voice of* MRS. PEPYS *comes shrill.*)

MRS. PEPYS. Samuel, where have you been ?
PEPYS. At the Navy Office, my love . . .

(MRS. PEPYS *sits.*)

(BOY *enters.*)

—doing the King's work ! Here, boy, my hat ! my stick ! Make haste !

(*The* BOY *takes his things.* PEPYS *turns, clapping his hands together and rubbing them with forced heartiness, and sits head of table.*)

Faith, I'm mighty glad to see ye all, mighty glad, upon my soul.
MRS. PEPYS. *All* this time at the office ?
PEPYS. Every minute, my treasure . . . Gad, I'd forgotten.

(*Taking a parcel from his pocket, rising and going below table to* MRS. PEPYS.) Not every minute ; I slipped round to Unthanke's and knocked 'em up to get you this. (*He puts a beautiful lace scarf round her shoulders and kisses her. She turns her head from the kiss.*)

MRS. PIERCE. My, what a beauty!

HUMFREY. *Amende honorable!*

MRS. PEPYS (*pulling the scarf from her shoulders*). And what is this in honour of—the launching of *The Great Beare*?

PEPYS (*returning above table to his seat*). Nay, she's still in the slips . . . 'tis to cover your pretty bare shoulders, my love.

(*He sits at the head of table as* DOLL *hurries from the kitchen with the dish of veal and sets it in front of him.*)

DOLL. A mighty fine breast of veal, hot as the debil. (*Then in a loud whisper.*) An' I keep de lil' ole hare all for you, massa, with prune sauce.

PEPYS. Nay, I will but clap a bit of meat in my mouth. (*Attacking the veal.*)

(PELLING *pours out wine for him.*)

I'm mighty glad you did not wait for me.

MRS. PIERCE. Oh, we did wait . . . but 'twas for Mistress Pepys. (*Giggles.*)

MRS. KNEPP. Who came not home till ten.

PEPYS (*feigning amazement*). Not home till ten, my love?

MRS. PEPYS (*sharply*). I had business . . . which kept me abroad.

PEPYS. Business?

MRS. PEPYS (*fiercely*). Ay, business!

MRS. PIERCE (*to* PEPYS). And would not tell us what . . . sly puss! (*Looking at* MRS. PEPYS *and shaking her finger at her.*)

MRS. PEPYS. Madam, 'twas no one's business but mine.

PEPYS. Nay, nay, but to let our guests shift for themselves till ten o' the clock.

HUMFREY. *Pardie!* Monsieur Pepys, we were well amused. I sang them songs—we sang together—and the ladies were charming. (*Bowing to* MRS. PIERCE.)

MRS. PIERCE (*with a squeal of delight*). Oh, Mr. Humfrey, but you're hugeously gallant.

MRS. KNEPP (*loudly*). Let's sing again, faith—"Marry me now." Come on, Cæsar!

(MRS. KNEPP *sings the first six lines, then all except* MRS. PEPYS *take up the refrain:* "Marry me now, marry me now, marry me, marry me now.")

SONG: "Marry Me Now."

"Said Brawny Bill, the sailor bold,
   Oh, marry me now!
Our love is nearly two days old,
   Marry me, marry me now!

I've got the parson and the ring,
I mean to do the proper thing.
  Marry me now, marry me now,
  Marry me, marry me now.

" You see I've got to sail away,
  Oh, marry me now !
I'd hate to miss my wedding day,
  Marry me, marry me now !
For life is short and love is long,
And once we're spliced we can't go wrong.
  Marry me now, marry me now,
  Marry me, marry me now !

PELLING. Marry me now——

" Heave to, my lass, and strike your sail,
  Oh, marry me now !
A sailor lad will never fail !
  Marry me, marry me now,
You may not see him once a year,
But when he's there he'll make you cheer.
  Marry me now, marry me now !
  Marry me, marry me now ! "

(The refrain gets more and more noisy, till at last MRS. PIERCE *screams it, beating time on the table with a spoon.)*

MRS. PEPYS *(suddenly springing up).* Have done ! Have done ! Have done ! I tell you ! . . . Will ye drive me mad ?
HUMFREY. *Pauvre Madame Pepys !*
MRS. KNEPP. What have *I* done ?
MRS. PIERCE. We do but sing !
PEPYS. What is it, wife ? *(Rising.)*

(All rise.)

MRS PEPYS *(going to the foot of stairs).* My head ! . . . My head ! . . . the caterwauling . . . send 'em away, I can't bear it . . . I can't . . . I can't !
PEPYS. Nay, wife, what's amiss, my love ? *(Coming to her.)*

(Mrs. PEPYS turns with a fierce whisper.)

MRS. PEPYS. Don't you dare to come near me ! *(Aloud, going up the stairs.)* I beg you'll pardon me . . . I am not well—I think I am not well . . . I must to bed . . . good night . . . good night !
PELLING. Good night !
MRS. KNEPP. *Good* night ! *(Laughing softly.)*
HUMFREY. *Je suis désolé, chère Madame Pepys, bon soir !*
MRS. PIERCE *(coming o., leering).* Abroad till ten—fie ! fie !
MRS. KNEPP. Hush !

(MRS. PEPYS *disappears into the room above.*)

PEPYS. Faith, I misdoubt but her mind's in a toss about something, poor wretch ! 'Twere best we *all* say good night . . .

PELLING. Fait¹ so !

HUMFREY (*coming down* L.). *Je crois bien, pauvre petite !*

PEPYS. We'll hold this feast some other night. Take away, girls ! Boy Jacke ! Attend the door.

(*The* GIRLS *begin clearing the table. The* BOY *goes out.*)

HUMFREY (*taking up his cithern and coming* C. *to* PEPYS). *Bon soir,* M. Pepys. I could not sing to-night. *Ma foi, non !* The mood is gone.

MRS. PIERCE. Nay, nay, come to my house and Babs and Cæsar. We'll be merry yet. (*Giggles, then going to* PEPYS.) Something has happened, take my word. (*Pointing upstairs.*)

PEPYS. Faith, very like.

MRS. PIERCE. Good night, sweet man ! (*Holding out her cheek.*)

PEPYS (*shaking her hand*). Good night. (*He leaves her and crosses to the head of table.*)

MRS. PIERCE. Beast ! Come, *dear* Mr. Humfrey ! (*Turning.*) Merry yet, i' faith ! (*She begins to dance, singing.*) " Marry me now, marry me now, marry me——"

ALL. Hush ! hush ! hush ! hush

(MRS. PIERCE *goes out giggling.*)

HUMFREY (*following*). *Pardie !* The cream is turned to butter . . .

(*Goes out laughing, followed by* CÆSAR.)

MRS. KNEPP (*who has crossed* R., *in a whisper*). Good night, thou naughty knave !

PEPYS (*kissing her*). Good night, thou saucy wench !

(MRS. KNEPP *goes out.*)

(*To* PELLING, *who is following.*) Pelling, is there ne'er a medicine to keep a woman quiet ?

PELLING. Faith, yes . . . but I cannot sell it you. (*Turning to door.*)

PEPYS. What ?

PELLING (*in doorway*). Just think, friend Pepys ; good night ! (*Goes out.*)

PEPYS. Good night ! (*He stands looking after them.*)

(*The* GIRLS *have cleared the table of all save the candelabra, and are gone. Murmurs and soft laughter from the departing guests.* MRS. PIERCE *begins to sing again,* " Marry me now," *and is hushed down ;* PEPYS *says a second good night. Street door bang ; more soft laughter, then the sound of the* Boy *sliding the bolts of the door. They all start singing first verse of "Marry Me Now," which dies away in distance.* Pepys *turns and stands, gazing at the ground a moment. In the silence outside* Mrs. Pierce's *"Marry me now," then laughter and voices moving away.* Pepys *looks up at the bedroom door, hesitates a moment, then moves down to the foot of the stairs. He hesitates again. In the distance the refrain and laughter. He is about to mount the stairs, then stands thinking a moment and goes to the cupboard* R. *Far away the "Marry me now" and faint laughter.* Pepys *takes the newly acquired Bible from the cupboard, goes and sits at the head of the table. For a moment he sits thinking, then sighs and opens the Bible and begins to read. The door upstairs opens softly.* Mrs. Pepys *comes to the balustrade and looks down. She is in petticoat and dressing-jacket, soft slippers on her feet and a lace cap on her head. She turns and comes noiselessly down the stairs, comes a little way towards him, then stands watching him. A pause.)*

Mrs. Pepys (*in a low voice*). I'm sorry . . . I flew out . . . before 'em all.

Pepys. Wife! (*He rises to go to her. She stretches out her hands to keep him away.*)

Mrs. Pepys. You should have been home.

Pepys (*sitting*). I know.

(*A pause.*)

Mrs. Pepys. Where were you?

Pepys. I told you.

(*She is silent.*)

At the Navy Office.

Mrs. Pepys (*she shuts her mouth grimly and shakes her head and crosses* R. *to chest*). Why did you bring me the scarf?

Pepys. To please you.

Mrs. Pepys. Humph!

Pepys. Faith, there's no pleasing you! Did you not ask for it to-day?

Mrs. Pepys. I did. And you said you'd think——

Pepys. And I did think, and thought to please you, and went round and knocked Unthanke out of bed for it. Cost me four pounds eighteen.

Mrs. Pepys. Ay, conscience money! (*Sits on chest.*)

Pepys. What d'ye mean?

Mrs. Pepys. When you gave me the scarf, then I knew there was something wrong. And you so agreeable, too . . . with my love, and my pet, and my treasure——

Pepys (*nettled*). Faith, I shan't be agreeable much longer.

Mrs. Pepys. There's a certain smile—how well I know it!

(PEPYS *removes his glasses.*)

When I see it oozing on your face, I'm sure you've been up to some roguery. (*A pause.*) Where were you ?

PEPYS.   How many times do you want to hear it ? . . . At the Navy Office.

MRS. PEPYS.   It's a lie !

PEPYS.   Woman, are you out o' your wits ?   Ask the boy there, if you don't believe me.

MRS. PEPYS.   I have asked him already.

PEPYS.   Well, and what did he tell you ?

MRS. PEPYS.   At the Navy Office. (*Imitating* BOY.)

PEPYS.   Of course he did.

MRS. PEPYS.   Yes, of course !   He saw you go in, and he didn't see you come out.   But I know better—I know you lied to me before you went out, and I know you're lying now.

PEPYS (*springing up and shouting*).   I told you I was going to the Navy Office, and that is where I've been !

MRS. PEPYS (*springing up*).   Navy Office be damned ! . . . You lied about Lettice !   I saw you kiss her, and you lied and said you didn't, and the moment you were gone I had her in and she confessed.

PEPYS.   Pooh !   You frightened her——

MRS. PEPYS.   I frightened the truth out of her, wretch !

PEPYS.   Truth !   Pshaw !   A silly green girl, frighted out of her life. . . .   What could she know of the truth ?   Pish, talk sense ! I might have brushed against her lips by accident, when looking down her throat, and she, poor fool, she *thought* it was a kiss.   And here *you* come making all this great ado about naught (*moving up to* MRS. PEPYS), and I only waiting to learn what *you* were doing that kept you abroad till ten . . . ay, madam, till ten o' the clock, gadding by night . . . in the City . . . alone !   Were you alone ?

MRS. PEPYS.   Yes.

PEPYS.   Why did ye not take one of the maids with you ?

MRS. PEPYS (*crossing down* R.).   Because I didn't choose !

PEPYS.   Ay, didn't choose they should see where you went and what you did—I'll be bound you didn't !   But *I* mean to know ! . . . Choose or no choose . . . your husband has got to learn the truth !   Speak, woman—where went you ?

MRS. PEPYS.   After you to the Navy Office—(*flying out*)—and you weren't there !

PEPYS.   I *was* there !

MRS. PEPYS.   I knocked and knocked till my hands ached——

PEPYS.   I heard ye not.   What time was it ?

MRS. PEPYS.   After seven, maybe.

PEPYS.   And you stood three hours knocking at the Navy Office !

MRS. PEPYS.   No . . . I went—— (*She hesitates.*)

PEPYS.   Where ?   Where ?

Mrs. Pepys.   To Mistress Knight's . . . the singing woman . .
to look for you.

Pepys.   Look for me, indeed !   What should take *me* there ?

Mrs. Pepys (*taking the paper from her breast*).   That !   I found it
there on the table.

Pepys (*taking it*).   'Tis none o' mine.

Mrs. Pepys.   I saw you search for it before you went——

Pepys.   Fiddle faddle !   I searched for a sheet of music. (*Crump-
ling it into a ball and putting it in his pocket.*)   Jealous whimsies to
turn me from the truth !   But you can't deceive me ! . . .   Come,
out with it !   What were you doing, and who were you with ?

Mrs. Pepys (*sullenly*).   With Mistress Knight.

Pepys.   Alone ?

(She is silent.)

Answer me ! . . .   Who else was there ?

(No reply.)

Woman, do you hear . . . who else ?

Mrs. Pepys.   The . . . the King.

Pepys.   The King !   Hell and devils !   You . . . my wife . . .
with the King . . . all that time with the King !

Mrs. Pepys.   No, no—not all that time !

Pepys.   Faith, long enough to make a naught of you !

Mrs. Pepys.   No, Samuel, no . . . he was mighty civil to
me——

Pepys.   Oh, mighty civil !   I'll wager he was.   Faith, I know
his civility . . . and you'll be on the civil list before we know . . .
ay, madam . . . a royal mistress . . . (*crossing down* L.) and lead
me about as consort in a crown of horns !

Mrs. Pepys (*going on her knees*).   No . . . no . . . no . . . I
swear not !

Pepys.   Heaven grant me patience !   (*Pretending to swallow his
rage.*)   But come . . . I'll be calm . . . I'll be calm . . . if I
can . . . I'll question you quietly. (*Standing over her.*)   Yes . . .
that's the way . . . on your knees . . . mighty proper . . . and
we'll have the truth . . . at last.   Come now, tell me what happened
. . . confess it all ! . . . I can bear it . . . I can bear anything,
so it be the truth.   He made love to you . . . eh ?

Mrs. Pepys.   No !

Pepys.   What ?

Mrs. Pepys.   No, no, Samuel !

Pepys.   He played with you ? . . . Kissed you . . . eh ?

Mrs. Pepys.   No, Samuel, no, he didn't !

Pepys.   I want the truth.

Mrs. Pepys.   He did me no wrong, I swear it.

Pepys.   What *did* he do ?

MRS. PEPYS. He . . . he talked to me.

PEPYS. Faith! I wouldn't believe that if a bench of bishops swore it. Talked to you! Could he be five minutes with a pretty woman in a room and keep his hands off her?—Not if they were tied behind his back! (*Going up* R.)

MRS. PEPYS. It's the truth, Samuel, the truth!

PEPYS (*coming to her*). Oh, woman, woman! And here am I, poor, honest, sober man, going my ways about my business . . while my wife is dallying with the King. (*He turns away to* L.)

MRS. PEPYS (*beginning to cry*). I am true to you, Samuel . . . I am. I've always . . . been . . . true to you . . . always . . . no ma-ma-ma-matter who tried to tempt me. (*She hides her face in her hands.*)

(PEPYS *turns, realizing he has gone too far.*)

PEPYS. Don't cry . . . (*Going to her.*) Come, don't cry . . . I'll believe you. . . . Faith, I know you're true. (*Raising her up and patting her back.*) Don't cry . . . I can't bear to see you cry. Come, wife . . . come . . . sit you here. . . . (*He seats her in his chair at the head,* R. *end, of the table.*) That's better . . . and we won't cry any more . . . eh?

(*She brushes away her tears with her fingers.*)

That's better . . . ay . . . I know you're true to me, but I know likewise you're not to be trusted with liberty—what woman is?— for away from me you're but a fool. And I would have this night a lesson to you . . . ay . . . against jealousy and vain imaginings . . . plaguing me with your suspicions, and all that would make a hell of our home. Come, promise you'll never suspect me again.

MRS. PEPYS (*looks at him*). I promise.

PEPYS. Nay, before we lie in our bed to-night, swear it me as a vow. . . . Faith! here's the Book at your elbow. (*Moves to* L. *of* MRS. PEPYS *above table and closes Bible.*) Put your hand upon it.

(*She puts her hand on the Book.*)

So! . . . now repeat the words after me: "I, Elisabeth Pepys . . ."

(*The sound of horses' hoofs coming nearer is heard.*)

MRS. PEPYS. I, Elisabeth Pepys . . .

PEPYS. "Do hereby swear that never again . . .'

MRS. PEPYS. Do hereby swear that never again . . .

PEPYS. "Will I suspect my husband . . ."

MRS. PEPYS. Will I suspect my husband . . .

PEPYS. " Whatsoever he may say or do "—

(*Stop horses' hoofs.*)

" or others may say against him . . ."

MRS. PEPYS. Whatsoever he may say——

(*The horses with a great clatter pull up outside the house. They are both silent, listening. A thunderous knocking on the door.*)

PEPYS (*after a pause*). What can that be ?

MRS. PEPYS (*aghast*). At this hour ! (*She rises.*)

PEPYS (*going up*). Boy, boy, Jacke ! Wake up !

(*He throws a boot down the passage. Another loud knock.*)

MRS. PEPYS (*who has stolen up to the window, pressing her face against the glass*). The King's liveries !

PEPYS. The King's !

MRS. PEPYS. What could it mean ? (*Coming down.*) War ? War with the Dutch ?

PEPYS. The Dutch—the devil ! (*Going down* L.)

(*Two bolts withdrawn.*)

(PRODGERS *enters solemnly bearing on a velvet cushion the flageolet. He comes* C. *and with a stately bow to* MRS. PEPYS.)

PRODGERS. His Majesty sends his warmest greetings to Mistress Pepys, and commands me to deliver this instrument into her hands. (*He comes down to* MRS. PEPYS *and holds out the cushion to* MRS. PEPYS, *who wonderingly takes the flageolet.*) His Majesty desires that you will keep jealous guard upon it, madam, as he has observed that Mr. Pepys' love of music leads him to leave it about in strange places. (*Then, putting the cushion under his arm, he bows to each.*) Madam ! . . . Mr. Pepys !

(*He stalks out. Street door bang. Two bolts.* PEPYS *stands looking as if he wished the earth would swallow him. The clattering of the horses' hoofs dies away in the distance.* MRS. PEPYS *stands staring at the flageolet in her hand.*)

MRS. PEPYS (*in a low dazed voice*). How came this here ? . . . You took it out . . . I saw it. . . . The King ! . . . You were there ! . . . at Mistress Knight's. . . . You were there !

PEPYS (*stammering*). I . . . was at . . . the Navy Office . . . I——

MRS. PEPYS. Don't give me that raggedy lie again . . . you were there ?

(*He is silent. She goes on, deadly quiet.*)

The truth . . . or I walk out of your house to-night !

PEPYS. It's true . . . I *was* there.

MRS. PEPYS. All the time ?

PEPYS. All the time.

MRS. PEPYS. Where ?

PEPYS (*quickly*). Not in the bedroom.

MRS. PEPYS. No, I know you weren't . . . Where ?

PEPYS. In the c-curtains——

MRS. PEPYS. A lie ! The King was there.

PEPYS. Behind the other ones.

MRS. PEPYS. So ! . . . You black-mouthed liar, is that the truth, at last ?

PEPYS (*nodding*). At last.

MRS. PEPYS. And you made *me* confess, you rotten-hearted rogue ! . . . you forgave *me* . . . made *me* swear vows . . . you pricklouse ! you unmitigated monster ! (*Stalks towards* PEPYS.) And all the time you were false to me with that woman !

(*She springs at him, beating him with the flageolet. He backs, trying to ward off the blows with his arms.*)

False to me ! . . . Dog ! . . . False to me ! . . . You hound ! You lying hound ! . . . False ! . . . False ! . . . False, you stinking devil !

(*He succeeds in catching her wrists ; they struggle, swaying.*)

PEPYS. I wasn't false !

MRS. PEPYS. Liar !

PEPYS. I went to hear her sing.

MRS. PEPYS. Lies !

PEPYS. I went to make music——

MRS. PEPYS (*freeing her right hand and grabbing the flageolet from the left, holds it back to strike*). All lies !

PEPYS (*throwing off her left hand and retreating*). It's true ! Look at the proof in your hand.

MRS. PEPYS (*flinging it at him*). A lie !

PEPYS (*shouting*). Woman, it's true ! And didn't *you* lie to *me* ?

MRS. PEPYS. I didn't.

PEPYS (*coming to her, furious*). You did ! You let the King make love to you—I heard him.

MRS. PEPYS. I couldn't stop him !

PEPYS. And he tickled you !

MRS. PEPYS. I couldn't help it !

PEPYS. And you liked it !

MRS. PEPYS. No, I didn't.

PEPYS. Yes, you did, you laughed !

MRS. PEPYS. I *must* laugh when I'm tickled.

PEPYS. And worse—he kissed you.

MRS. PEPYS. You know that ?

PEPYS. Know it, woman !—you were sitting on top of me !

MRS. PEPYS. Samuel ! (*Staring at him.*) You were in the chest !

(*He hangs his head, ashamed.*)

Oh, Samuel, how undignified !

(*She sinks into the chair at the head of the table, then after a pause, struggling with her tears.*)

What are we to do ? . . .   What are we to do ? . . .   How can we ever live together again . . . after . . . to-night ! (*Sobbing.*)

PEPYS (*frightened*). You don't mean that ? (*Starts moving towards her.*) . . . You don't *really* mean that ?

MRS. PEPYS. But I *do* mean it . . . I *must* mean it.

PEPYS. Don't say that. . . . (*He comes over behind the table, beginning to cry.*) You couldn't, wife, you couldn't say that. (*He sits a little away from her leaning his arms on the table.*)

MRS. PEPYS (*sobbing*). But I must say it . . . how can I ever believe you again !

PEPYS (*sobbing*). I can promise . . . never to lie to you.

MRS. PEPYS (*sobbing*). But I couldn't *believe* it.

(*A pause broken by sobs.*)

And . . . to think . . . that you were there . . . all the time !

PEPYS (*sobbing*). Yes . . . all the time.

(*A slight pause.*)

MRS. PEPYS (*sobbing*). If you knew . . . what I was suffering . . . in my heart !

PEPYS (*sobbing*). If you knew . . . what I was suffering . . . in the chest ! (*He takes out his handkerchief and wipes his eyes.*)

MRS. PEPYS (*sobbing*). But you . . . *deserved* it.

PEPYS (*sobbing*). Yes . . . yes . . . I deserved it.

(*She wipes away the tears with her fingers. He passes her the handkerchief.*)

MRS. PEPYS (*sobbing*). How can I ever know now . . . that you weren't false . . . with that woman ?

PEPYS (*sobbing*). I could . . . swear I wasn't.

MRS. PEPYS (*sobbing*). Yes . . . but what's . . . the good ?

(*He is wiping tears away with his fingers. She passes the handkerchief.*)

PEPYS (*sobbing*). I could swear it on the Book . . . there's a mighty difference . . . between general swearing . . . and swearing on the Book.

MRS. PEPYS (*sobbing a little*). Is there ?

PEPYS. A mighty difference.

MRS. PEPYS. Very well . . . put your hand on it   . . swear it on the Book.

(*He puts his hand on the Book.*)

PEPYS. I swear . . . I was never . . . naught with Knight.

WATCHMAN (*in the distance outside*). Past twelve o' the clock, and a fine windy morning!

MRS. PEPYS. Now swear . . . you will never see her again.

PEPYS. I swear I will never see her again . . . if I can help it.

MRS. PEPYS (*quickly*). *No, no, no,* you *must* help it.

PEPYS (*quickly*). But how can I help it ?   I might see her at the play, at Court, in the street.   Would you have me forswear myself ?

WATCHMAN (*a little nearer*). Past twelve o' the clock and a fine windy morning.

MRS. PEPYS (*rising*). Then you must swear to shut your eyes.

PEPYS. I swear if I see her I will shut my eyes.

MRS. PEPYS (*going to* C.). And now one more, Samuel . . . swear that you will never look at a pretty woman again.

(*He puts his hand on the Book.*)

PEPYS. I swear I will never look at a pretty woman again—and may the Lord help me to keep that vow.

MRS. PEPYS. Amen ! (*Crosses* R. *and blows out candle on chest— then down to foot of stairs.*) Bring the light, Samuel.

WATCHMAN (*far away*). Past twelve o' the clock and a fine windy morning.

(SAMUEL, *who has followed her with the candlestick from table, stands beside the staircase watching her go up.*)

PEPYS. Wife !

(*She stops and looks at him, then leaning over the banisters, bends down and kisses him.* PEPYS *follows her upstairs.*)

And so to bed !

CURTAIN.

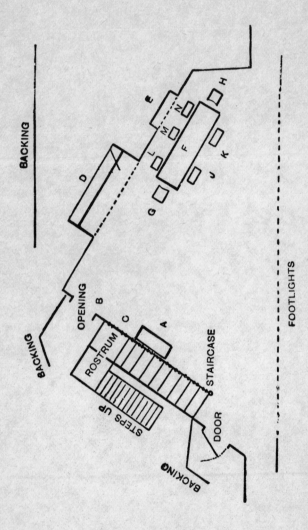

PROPERTY AND FURNITURE PLOT

ACTS I AND III

Stage cloth parquet flooring to cover the whole stage.

F. A long Cromwellian table L.C.

L. M. N. 3 stools behind table.

J. K. 2 stools are in front of the table.

G. H. A chair is at either end of the table.

D. In the centre of the room in the back wall is a deeply embrasured Tudor window with a step up from floor-level, a seat running around same.

A. A large oak chest is set up and down by the staircase, which is R.

Silver candlesticks and pewter pots and plates are on chest when scene opens, with cleaning materials for SUE, for cleaning same.

An old pewter and a bowl, to throw from window, are placed on settle to open.

Tapestry covers the walls to about half-way up.

E Book-shelves are inset behind the tapestries on the wall behind table. In these shelves are a number of books, papers, music, etc.

On table is an ink pot and quill pen.

4 loose sheets of paper.

Music and flageolet.

Flagon of wine off R.

Satchel for papers.

Stick.

Knocker and bolts to work off R.

Water in bowl.

Feather and lighted taper.

Handkerchief for business.

Bible and 3 play books.

Cithern in bag and another similar (lute) instrument

List of accounts for DOLL.

Cushion for King's Messenger (Act III).

Dishes of various kinds and shapes.

Plates, knives, forks, spoons, etc.

2 wooden Trays for maids.

Silver flagon, glasses, etc., for the supper scene.

Hare for DOLL, with one hind leg jointed, ready to out for business.

Hare's foot for PEPYS.

B. Opening to hall.

C. Recessed bookcase in wall under landing.

71

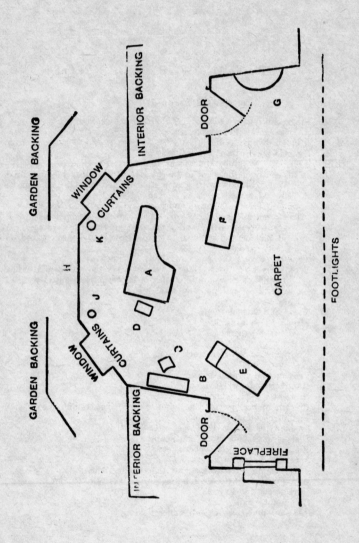

GARDEN BACKING

GARDEN BACKING

INTERIOR BACKING

INTERIOR BACKING

WINDOW

WINDOW

CURTAINS

CURTAINS

DOOR

DOOR

FIREPLACE

CARPET

FOOTLIGHTS

A

B

C

D

E

F

G

H

J

K

ACT II

A. Harpsichord, with candle lighted on c. of same.
Key in lock of R. door.
Heavy curtains to close and work at both windows up c.
Pelmets to same.
Pictures on walls. Portrait of King Charles II over fireplace.
B. Dressing-table, with looking-glass, table-cover, pots, etc.
C. Chair, high-backed, at dressing-table.
Fender, fire-irons.
J. K. 2 large lamps by windows.
Candle lighted on dressing-table.
Candle lighted on table down L.
Music about on harpsichord.
D. Stool at harpsichord.
E. Day-bed sofa R.C.
Cushions, etc., for same.
F. A large Italian Renaissance marriage chest.
Green stockings (silk), music and flageolet for PEPYS.
G. Side-table, with lighted candle on same.
H. Picture of Venus.

Any character costumes or wigs needed in the performance of this play can be hired from Charles H. Fox Ltd, 184 High Holborn, London W C 1

LIGHTING PLOT

ACT I

Amber and reds in floats and battens—not too full, say ¾ up.
Bright amber flood outside window on backing.
Length under arch.—Amber and red, 2 lamps of each.
Length at outside door down R.—2 amber lamps.
Perches.—Amber and red mixed. Open limes. Remain through Act.

ACT II

Ambers—Floats and battens. FULL UP.
Lengths outside doors R. *and* L.—2 reds, 2 ambers in each.
Fire lighted.
1st Check.—When MRS. KNIGHT rises and blows out candle on the harpsichord.
2nd Check.—As MRS. KNIGHT takes candle from down L. and closes bedroom door L.
3rd Check.—As KING CHARLES goes into bedroom.

Curtain—Black Out.

Lights up for Call.

ACT III

Ambers and reds in floats and battens—FULL UP.
Perches.—Open limes, amber.
Blue flood outside window on back cloth.
Length off at outside arch up R.—Red 2 lamps and 1 amber.
Length at outside door down R.—2 amber lamps.
1st Check.—As tray with candles is removed.
2nd Check.—As MRS. PEPYS blows out candle on settle R.
3rd Check.—PEPYS takes candle and watches her up the stairs.
4th Check.—As PEPYS goes off with candle through door at the top of stairs.

Curtain—Black Out.

Lights up for Call.